Quiltmaking

BY CATHERINE FALLIN

GROSSET
GOOD LIFE
BOOKS

PUBLISHERS . GROSSET & DUNLAP . NEW YORK
A FILMWAYS COMPANY

Photographs by Catherine Fallin
Drawings by Maryweld Luhrs
Cover photograph by Mort Engel

Copyright © 1977 by Grosset & Dunlap, Inc.
All rights reserved
Published simultaneously in Canada
Library of Congress catalog card number: 76-46741
ISBN 0-448- 12991-4 (trade edition)
ISBN 0-448- 13420-9 (library edition)
First printing

Printed in the United States of America

Contents

Introduction

Quiltmaking is a wonderful hobby. It requires no intricate skills or techniques other than basic sewing; yet any needlework craft can be applied to quiltmaking as embellishment. Making a quilt is as simple or as complicated as you want to make it. There are thousands of traditional patterns to follow for those who are fascinated by geometric shapes and their endless combinations. Even more possibilities exist if you want to design your own quilt.

Quilting is a delightfully inexpensive hobby and can be done anywhere. You don't need a studio or even a separate workroom. Since no special equipment is needed, you can make a quilt wherever you are.

A quilt can be a project as small as a pillow or a wall hanging that can be done in a few hours; or it can be a long-term project if you want to make a king-sized bedspread. Quiltmaking is one of the most personalized crafts that exists, since no two quilts are alike. Even if a traditional pattern is followed, the selection of fabrics and colors, the size of the blocks and individual pieces, and method of quilting all give each quilt its own special look. And, most importantly, quiltmaking is fun.

Two separate skills are involved in making a quilt. The first of the two is the creation of the top. This is the part of quiltmaking most often associated with the craft. The top can be either pieced or appliquéd. Traditionally, the pieced top was the most practical: it allowed the quiltmaker to make something new and beautiful from leftover scraps of new cloth or from old clothes too worn out to mend further but with good strong fabric still left in them. By piecing together tiny pieces into a larger pattern, a large bedcover could be made. When that top was backed with other fabric and both layers lined or stuffed with cotton or an old wool blanket, you not only had a beautiful cover but a very warm one as well.

Appliquéd quilt tops, on the other hand, were as much for the purpose of creating pretty designs and a decorative cover as they were for the practicality of recycling leftover fabric. More appliquéd quilts were made from new cloth with the same colors repeated in the overall design than were made from scraps. Appliquéd quilts were often made to commemorate a special occasion, such as a wedding, or for presentation to a local dignitary. Many times a group of people would collaborate on one quilt, with each person making one square.

One member would join the squares, and then the whole group would gather at a quilting bee to quilt the layers together.

The Bicentennial provided an occasion for many groups to make quilts both to record the history of localities and to commemorate the occasion. But even these luxurious appliquéd quilts were joined to a backing and usually filled with an inner layer of material for warmth.

Warmth brings us to the second practical function of a quilt, as well as to the second skill involved in quiltmaking. That is the quilting itself. The word *quilt* can refer to the whole finished cover or just to the top. Quilting is the method of stitching together all the layers so that they won't come apart. It also adds strength to the quilt. The method and pattern of the quilting stitching has become a fine art of its own. There are endless antique patterns of flowers, bouquets, wreaths, feathers, harps, eagles, and anything else you can imagine.

This book is written for anyone who would like to make a quilt—any kind or style of quilt, traditionally by hand or quickly by machine, for any size bed from a crib to a king-sized bed. It supplies all the information you need to plan your quilt, select its fabrics, measure and cut, make the patterns, adapt old patterns to new methods, and estimate amounts of fabric. Instructions are given step by step from your first planning to your last quilting stitch.

Instructions are given for very simple quilts and more difficult projects. You can make any of the quilts exactly as illustrated or adapt it to your own size or style. Specific directions are given for both hand sewing and machine stitching. Alternate ways of proceeding or choices of materials needed are given wherever practical.

The first part of the book is devoted to the pertinent descriptions of methods and materials you need to know about before you make your first quilt. The skills and facts necessary for making a quilt are not difficult in themselves, but they can be difficult to find. As with any hobby, everyone acquires his or her own preferred ways of working and favorite supplies through experience. I have tried to list as many hints and alternate suggestions as possible and have often given other quiltmaker's preferences as well as my own.

The second part of the book gives detailed instructions for specific patterns. There is a good cross section of sizes, designs, quilts easily done by machine or hand. I have listed the total number of pieces needed for each quilt, the finished dimensions of the example of the pattern illustrated, and the best method for assembling the basic block, as well as the quilt as a whole. The amounts of fabric needed are given in both 36-inch and 45-inch fabric widths. Patterns of quilting are suggested. A photograph of the entire quilt is given, as well as detailed drawings of pattern pieces and blocks.

The intention of this book is to make quiltmaking as simple and enjoyable a hobby as I have found it, and I have tried to answer for you all the questions I had when I first began making quilts.

Wild Goose Chase. Pieced quilt (1353 pieces) made by Elizabeth Roper Fallin, c. 1915. Quilt courtesy Margaret Fallin Guinn.

Part I
General Instructions

This delightful scene is appliquéd from hand drawn patterns and highlighted by the quilting stitches. Notice the waves on the lake created by the quilting. Quilt courtesy The Hired Hand.

1
Planning Your Quilt

Now that you have decided to make a quilt, the first thing to do is to plan the kind of quilt that you want. You must decide what purpose the quilt will serve, who the quilt is for, and how the quilt will be used.

The answers to these questions are essential, since they will determine the size, the pattern, and the colors of your quilt. Will the quilt be used for warmth as well as for a decorative covering for the bed? If warmth is important, be sure to bear that in mind when choosing the material for the filling of the quilt. What purpose will the quilt have? If it will be a bedspread, do you want it to come to the floor on all sides or just to the top of a dust ruffle? Do you know the size of the bed it will cover so you can plan its dimensions exactly? Or should you make the quilt a general size that can be used in several ways and on different beds? Will the quilt be used in place of a blanket under a spread? If so, you will want to make it large enough to tuck in at the foot and maybe on the sides. Will the quilt perhaps be used to cover an infant or a napping person?

If your quilt has a specific purpose and will be used in a particular room, consider the style of the furniture and the color of the walls and draperies. If the room is decorated with traditional furniture, almost any traditional patchwork or appliqué pattern is appropriate. However, you should be sure not to choose a pattern or combination of colors that conflicts with other patterns or colors in the room. For a more contemporary feeling, you can adapt the more traditional patterns by using only two or three colors instead of a large array of solid colors and prints. Many of the traditional appliqué patterns are particularly effective when worked in simple bright colors for a modern room.

Who will use the quilt? Are you making the quilt for an adult, for a teenager, for a newlywed couple, for a child, for yourself? Where will the quilt be used? If the quilt is a gift, it is advisable to choose a pattern that is flexible enough to adapt to several different decors. If you are making the quilt for a child's room, there is a vast range of delightful appliqué patterns to choose from. You may make a child's quilt small enough to be used only on a crib or to wrap the baby in. The quilt can be done in pastels with simple childish figures to delight a baby. On the other hand, you may decide on a somewhat more "grown-up" design for a child as well as a larger size that will last for many years. Pennsylvania Dutch designs with hearts and flowers and birds are very colorful and delightful, and they offer great adaptability for years of use. You can also create your own design. Free-form appliqué designs are great for children; to make the patterns for cutting, draw figures freehand on cardboard.

If you know what the quilt will be used for, where it will be used, and by whom, you can plan a very specific quilt. But if you don't know its specific purpose, perhaps it is better to keep the design a basic one that can be adapted for a variety of uses and places. The size can be made general as well.

Probably the most important consideration is the time it will take you to complete the project. If you have plenty of time, then feel free to choose any pattern regardless of how complicated or intricate it may be. But remember that your first quilt will take you longer to make because you will be experimenting with techniques and methods. After you are experienced in planning and making patterns, cutting, and sewing, you can work more complicated patterns more quickly and comfortably. It is generally better, then, for your first quilt to choose one of the simpler patterns or to adapt one of the more complicated ones to larger block sizes. If you think a small quilt for a baby or a small wall hanging is a simple project, remember that small overall dimensions do not shorten or simplify your project; you still must use either a pattern with only a few pieces per block or one with large block sizes.

Compare the baby quilt on page 76, which has 909 pieces, with the full-sized quilt on page 78, which has 527 pieces. To be more specific, the total number of pieces needed for your quilt determines how much time is needed to complete it, although there are ways to use the most intricate pattern in a workable length of time. For example, patterned blocks can be alternated with plain blocks, or patterned blocks can be joined with solid strips of fabric called lattice strips. Or the quilt can be enlarged by finishing it with one or more borders of variable widths. Moreover, the use of alternate plain blocks, lattice strips, or borders not only saves time but also highlights complicated block patterns that might well be lost if one intricately pieced block were joined to another intricate block without interruption of pattern.

You can simplify a very involved pattern by enlarging the size of the individual block. This means that each piece in the block will be larger and that fewer blocks will be needed, thereby reducing the total number of pieces in the quilt.

An old-fashioned quilt block was usually between 9 and 12 inches square. If a pattern has 20 pieces in each block and the quilt is a standard size for a double-bed blanket (84 × 96), made up of 12-inch blocks, that would be 7 blocks across and 8 down, for a total of 56 blocks to complete the top. To figure the total number of pieces in the quilt, multiply the number of blocks, 56, by the number of pieces, 20. This equals 1,120—a staggering number. If you increase your individual block size to 18 inches and you make a quilt 90 × 108 (dimensions increased to be evenly divisible by 18), you will need 5 blocks across and 6 down for a total of 30 blocks. Multiplied by 20 pieces per block, this means a quilt with only 600 pieces. Or if you take the original block size of 12 inches and use half patterned and half plain blocks, there will be a total of 588 pieces in the quilt (28 patterned blocks multiplied by 20 pieces plus 28 plain blocks). If you both increase block size to 18 inches and alternate patterned and plain blocks, you will have a quilt of 30 blocks; 15 patterned blocks multiplied by 20 pieces plus 15 plain blocks makes a total of 315 pieces. As you can see, this is a much simpler project than the original one, which required 1,120 pieces.

Another good method for deciding on a pattern or color scheme would be to make up a few "model" blocks, using a different pattern for each one. Those patterns you decide not to use can easily be made into pillows. Quilted pillows are lovely gifts for any occasion. If you have chosen a pattern that takes a long time merely to assemble one block, and if you multiply the time spent to make that block by the number of blocks in the finished quilt, you may decide on a less complicated pattern. Traditional patchwork or appliqué blocks vary from 3 pieces per block (Moon over the Mountain, for example) to as many as 40 or 50 pieces per block. Another hint: curved and circular pieces are more difficult and time-consuming to sew together than pieces with straight sides. Also, if you have a combination of pieces of approxi-

A Pennsylvania Dutch crib-sized appliquéd quilt. Quilt courtesy The Hired Hand.

mately the same size, it is easier and faster to sew them into a block than a variety of shapes and sizes.

Before estimating the amount of time it will take to make a quilt, decide whether you will piece it together by hand or by machine. Be forewarned that machine sewing is not necessarily a time-saver in piecing. Whether a pattern is suitable for machine sewing depends on the size of each piece, its shape, and the number of corners it has. Edges of less than 2 inches are usually more trouble to sew by machine than by hand. All corners must be sewn and matched exactly; machine corners are difficult to square unless you have had quite a bit of experience sewing. However, if your pieces are large enough (3 inches or more per side), machine piecing is the fastest method.

One of the advantages of making several blocks from different patterns is that it gives you a chance to experiment with various color combinations and patterns. You'll be able to see which one you like the best, you'll have an estimate of how long it will take to finish the quilt, and you'll have an idea as to the most suitable method for sewing it. When planning your quilt, remember, putting together the pieces to form each block is only the first step. After all the blocks have been made, they have to be sewn together to complete the top. Joining the blocks by machine is the fastest way. It also makes for quite secure stitching, but if you prefer to join your blocks by hand, make sure your stitches are small and, most importantly, even. Uneven stitches are much more likely to break under stress.

In some cases, it is also possible to do the actual quilting on a sewing machine. I recommend machine quilting for only the more simple and straight-lined quilting patterns, or for very small quilts with a thin layer of batting. Each time you stitch a row, the quilt must be taken away from the machine to refold it so that it will be flat and compact to fit between the needle and the body of the machine. It is not much easier or faster to use the sewing machine than it is to quilt by hand on a quilting frame. Once the quilt is attached to the frame, you simply stitch the quilting pattern and roll it each time you have finished quilting

a large portion. But everyone has a preferred method, and you'll discover your own in time. Some people would not quilt any other way than on a quilting frame, while others would use only a sewing machine. Still others prefer the quilting frame for basting the three layers together and then quilting by hand in their laps. There is no right or wrong way in quilting. Find whatever method is the simplest and most comfortable for you. I do most of my piecing by hand, especially for small pieces or combinations of shapes; I join the rows by machine and quilt by hand, using either a frame or an oversized embroidery hoop on a stand. Personally, I like the look of hand quilting much better than machine quilting. The quilting stitches are the ones that show on the finished product.

One more thing to consider when planning your quilt is what kind of fabric you want to use. The practical factors of sewing ease as well as care of the quilt are important. If a quilt is to be used for a bedcover, it will need to be cleaned more frequently than if it is hung on the wall; however, all quilts need to be cleaned or washed if you want to preserve them.

If the bedcover is to be used for a child, the quilt will need the most frequent washing of all. For children's quilts, I recommend using fabrics that are easily machine laundered and dried. This is not as obvious as it sounds. Fabrics should be nonshrinkable, colorfast, and of good quality so as not to fray or wear unevenly with frequent washings. You must also plan the fabric for the back of the quilt and the kind of batting or filler.

A great variety of colors and prints are available in 100-percent cotton and in cotton/polyester blends that can be easily machine washed and dried. Many of these washable fabrics, especially cotton, will get softer with continued use and washings, which only makes the quilt more lovely and comfortable.

If you are thinking of a quilt for purely decorative purposes, such as for a wall hanging, and are considering silks and/or satins, it is important to remember that although truly elegant, these quilts demand careful dry cleaning. Even if these quilts are hung as decoration, they will get dusty over time.

2
Design

You may want to coordinate the design for your quilt top with the design of your room. Decide if you want a traditional or a contemporary pattern. If you have traditional furniture, a traditional quilt pattern might blend with your room, but a contemporary pattern might give the room an interesting combination of styles. A contemporary pattern can simplify more ornate furnishings, and a traditional pattern can add color by visually softening the "straight line" of contemporary furniture. In other words, don't feel restricted to a particular style of quilt pattern by your choice of furniture; just be sure to coordinate the pattern of your quilt to complement the rest of your room. The real considerations are choice of pattern shapes, sizes, and colors. The relationship of the pattern to the colors of the quilt and the colors of the room is important. The pattern chosen for the quilt top is accented by the pattern of the quilting stitches chosen (see Quilting Methods, Ch. 13). The quilting stitches make their own pattern in relief over the pattern of the quilt top, adding depth and texture to the quilt as a whole. In addition, they serve the practical function of keeping the three layers of the quilt together and prevent the filling material from bunching up or shifting around.

Besides coordinating your quilt pattern to a room design, consider how the quilt will look on the bed. Part of the quilt will drape over the sides and bottom. So ask yourself whether you want your design to be centered only on the top of the bed or if you want it to continue over the edges.

Sources for Patterns

The selection of a pattern is purely subjective. Many first-time quilters have "always admired" a particular pattern and want to adopt that favorite for their first quilt. But before beginning, make a sample block to see how long it will take, and if necessary, simplify the pattern by one of the methods previously discussed.

If you don't have a favorite pattern, look at as many quilts as you can. You'll have a large number of patterns and color combinations to choose from. Visit galleries that display and sell quilts. Go to shops and museums and look at both new and antique quilts. Look through books of patterns. If you decide to copy a traditional quilt pattern, you needn't feel that your project has lost any creative value. The arrangement of the pattern and the color choices will personalize your quilt.

Patchwork Versus Appliqué

Patchwork is the art of joining small individual pieces of fabric cut into geometric shapes to make a larger geometric pattern, which in turn makes a quilt block. One block can make a whole quilt or several blocks can be joined together in various ways to make a quilt top.

Appliqué is the art of stitching pieces of fabric to the tops of other pieces of fabric, or overlaying fabric shapes on top of fabric backgrounds. Strictly speaking, appliqué is a variation of patchwork that has evolved into a separate kind of quilting all its own. In the early days of quilting in this country, patches were used to mend bedcovers and clothing. Sewing a piece of cloth over the worn or ripped part of the fabric is exactly the same as appliquéing. Both appliqué and patchwork are forms of modern quiltmaking that have existed ever since women began to create particular patterns for their quilts. The modern quilt is one done with a pattern in mind for decorative as well as practical effect.

Patchwork is most easily accomplished with pieces that have straight sides. Curved and circular designs are more readily adaptable to appliqué patterns. But patchwork and appliquéing are not mutually exclusive methods, and they are often combined in very lovely quilts.

Appliqué is most often used for intricately curved and irregularly shaped patterns, which can be achieved with fewer pieces than patchwork would need. Patterns created from nature motifs—such as flowers, birds, and animals—are usually done in appliqué because of their curves.

Patchwork motifs are usually derived from straight-sided geometric shapes—such as squares, rectangles, triangles, hexagons, octagons, diamonds, and stars—although gentle curves are sometimes used.

Choosing Patterns

Consider your experience with quilting, then choose a pattern you like a lot. Keep in mind the relationship and combination of lights and darks in the pattern and the colors you have chosen. One way of visualizing the shades is to draw the pattern on paper and shade it to get an overall effect. It is perfectly acceptable to use any combination of colors you wish, but remember that a quilt made up of several close shades may not show the pattern of little pieces within the block as well as strong light and dark contrasting colors. It will instead produce a very subtle pattern. Both strong contrasts and colors close in shade can be very pleasing, but they make for considerable difference in overall effect.

In other words, take into account the value of the colors you have chosen. Value in terms of color can best be defined as intensity. Contrasting colors may have the same value; for example, a quilt made of reds and blues of the same value will show up as the same shade of gray when photographed in black and white.

When deciding on your pattern, consider the texture of the fabrics, both literally and figuratively. The print of a fabric can imply a textured feeling that is not part of the fabric. The literal texture or feel of a fabric should also be considered from a practical standpoint. What may be pleasing to the eye or hand may be almost impossible to sew on or to use in combination with other fabrics.

Shapes

The degree of difficulty of your pattern is determined not only by the size and number of pieces used in a block, but also by the shapes of the pieces themselves and by the number of different shapes used within one block. For your first quilt, I again suggest simplicity. Although you needn't restrict yourself to only one shape, more than two or three shapes can get very complicated when it comes to sorting colors and pieces for individual blocks. Then there is the question of how much fabric you need, to say nothing of cutting and making patterns and keeping all your cut pieces sorted while working. As you increase your experience with

Moon over the Mountain.

It is an eye-catching pattern, largely because of its simplicity, but don't feel that a first quilt must be this simple. There are many patterns that are simple to work with but not simple in finished appearance. A Nine Patch is one of these patterns. Traditionally, it is done all in squares of the same size. But a basic Nine Patch of squares and triangles can make Jacob's Ladder as follows: the corner and center squares are themselves a Four Patch of alternating light and dark squares. The 4 alternating squares of the Nine Patch are each made up of 2 right triangles. A Churn Dash (a Nine Patch variation, sometimes called Sherman's March) is made up of 8 right triangles (all the same size) joined to make 4 squares for the corners, 8 small rectangles joined into 4 squares to form the centers of the outside rows, and 1 plain square in the middle of the block.

Windmill I, which is basically a Four Patch variation, is made up of 4 squares, each of which has 1 light and 1 dark right triangle. There are 8 triangles per block. When the 4 squares of 2 triangles are joined, they form the Windmill. Windmill II, or Pinwheel, is made

quilting, you will work out shortcuts and work habits that will simplify your work later.

The greater the number of shapes used, the more difficult it is to visualize your overall effect. It is best to keep to two shapes with no more than two sizes of each. One of the most simple patterns is Moon over the Mountain, which has only 3 pieces per block, including the background. It is made up of a circle and a triangle appliquéd onto a background square.

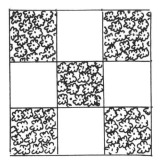 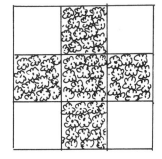 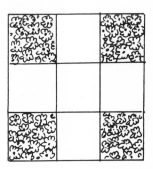

Simple Nine Patch variations.

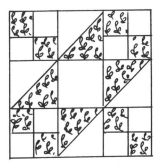 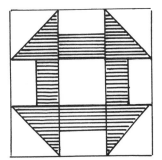 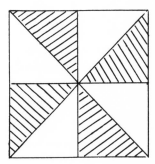

Jacob's Ladder.   *Churn Dash.*   *Windmill I.*

up of 12 right triangles (8 small and 4 large). Two small right triangles (1 light and 1 dark) are sewn together along two of the short sides to form a large right triangle; this new triangle is then sewn to the larger triangle, which can be the same color as the dark triangle or a third color, to form a square. The 4 squares are then joined to make a block as shown.

A Windmill is turned into Dutchman's Puzzle (another Four Patch variation) by using 8 large isosceles triangles of two colors and 16 right triangles all of one color joined together as follows. Two small triangles are sewn to the short sides of a larger triangle to form a rectangle. When 8 rectangles have been made, they are joined two at a time to form 4 squares, which are then arranged according to the illustration and sewn together to form the whole block.

As you can see, an endless number of combinations and patterns can be made simply by combining squares and triangles.

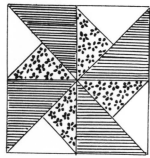

Windmill II (Pinwheel).

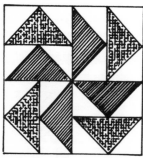

Dutchman's Puzzle.

Scale of Design

The scale of the design chosen for the top of the quilt should be geared to the individual room. Choose a common factor, either in a repeated shape or in a repeated color, that will tie the units of the quilt to one another as well as to the room the quilt will be in. If you are creating your own pattern, it is better to consider the shapes of your pieces first, then size, and then color.

You can have any number and combination of colors you like in your quilt. For instance, a medium blue, a white, and a red combine to create a very bright effect, the brightness depending on the shades of blue and red you have selected. You can change the overall effect of these same three colors if you sew several different prints of the same shade of blue and the same shade of red and make each block consistent with itself. If you take the same two colors in combination with white and alternate the use of red and blue blocks, you have still another effect. There have been quilts made from a different piece of fabric for each piece. I've seen one hexagon quilt where no one fabric is repeated; however, each piece in that quilt is exactly the same size and shape as its neighbor.

The point is that you can use any number of variables in putting together the pattern for the top of your quilt, but it is best to keep at least one common factor in your quilt, or you risk a very disturbing end result after many hours of work.

Planning Your Pattern

The key to favorable results is very careful planning before you begin your actual work. Plan all three design elements—size, shape, and color. When planning the design of the quilt top, consider the balance of both shapes and colors. There should not be a single piece or even a single block that dominates, distracts, or destroys the general balance of the quilt. If, for instance, you want to use a starkly contrasting color for accent, place it at regular intervals in the blocks (say in each block or in blocks that will be at regular intervals in the finished top). If you use a specially brilliant red, it could be placed at the center of a hexagon flower made up of several rings, or in every other hexagon in the quilt; then the quilt will be balanced. This is just one of many ways to bring balance to a design.

Planning your quilt is more than planning just the individual blocks. It is also planning how the blocks will fit together as a whole. Will a patterned block be joined to a patterned block? Or will the patterned blocks be alternated between plain blocks of a solid color or print? Or will the blocks be joined together with lattice strips? The process of joining the individual blocks together is called "setting" the quilt, and the pattern or arrangement of the joined blocks is called the "set."

Sometimes patterned blocks joined to patterned blocks can create new geometric patterns in the overall effect. For instance, Log Cabin blocks are made up of 13 or 17 rectangles radiating out from a central square, usually with an arrangement of light-colored and dark-colored pieces evenly balanced to one side or other of the block. Depending on how you arrange those light sides and dark sides when setting the top together, you can create variations of Log Cabin quilts called Barn Raising or Straight Furrow or Sunlight and Shadow.

Diamonds can be joined to form stars, such as Starry Crown or Lone Star (p. 82); or diamonds can be joined in groups of three to form a cube as in Baby Blocks (p. 65).

Sometimes patterned blocks are joined to solid color blocks, but one must be careful not to unbalance the quilt by having an uneven number of blocks in rows both across and down.

If you use solid-colored lattice strips to join the blocks, balance occurs almost naturally. But the balance can be lost if the blocks are of different rather than repeating colors and not arranged to balance the lighter ones. Lattice strips are narrow strips of fabric all of one color or print from 2 to 6 inches wide. They add continuity of color and shape and are often repeated as the border. Often lattice strips are cut wider when used as the border and thinner when used as in-between strips. They can be pieced if necessary to make them long enough or wide enough, but it is easier to use uniform lengths of fabric for strips sewn in one direction. The perpendicular direction will always have to be pieced. The width is usually determined by the proportionate width and length of the finished quilt. In other words, lattice strips are used as filler between the patterned blocks so that the quilt can be enlarged to the appropriate dimensions. Lattice strips also display each block by framing it. Traditionally, lattice strips are cut a consistent width throughout the quilt; otherwise, they would create their own pattern, perhaps conflicting with the patterned blocks. Additionally, they would not unify the quilt top if cut in different widths. Always take care in laying out patterned blocks before actually setting them together. Nothing is more disappointing than doing all the work of piecing and not being happy about the final arrangement of the blocks when they are finally joined together.

An even better plan is to lay out all the finished blocks on the floor and look at their arrangement. I have found that by moving the blocks around at this point, whole new patterns may reveal themselves. Finally, after you have decided on the best arrangement, mark the blocks in some fashion as you pick them up so you will remember the corresponding order in which to sew them together. This is particularly important if you have made a scrap quilt or a quilt with different colors predominating in each block. You can pin a numbered piece of paper to each block or you can write lightly on the wrong side of the block.

The final planning step is the border of the

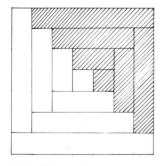

A Log Cabin block. Notice the arrangement of light and dark logs.

quilt, if you plan to have one. Sometimes a border is not decided on until the top has been completed; sometimes it is planned, although not specifically for overall size until the top is finished. A color or print in the pattern can be repeated in the border of the quilt. The border can function as a frame for the whole quilt or it can help balance a design. The border can also tie the quilt into the rest of the room. If you wish the border to unify the quilt and the room, it is most effective to repeat either a color or a print (or a variation) used elsewhere in the room. More than one border can be used to frame the quilt, giving you the freedom to enlarge the quilt at your discretion. If you have used a limited number of colors in the top, a repetition of two or three of these can be used in border strips. Borders too can serve the purpose of relating the color or pattern to the room in general by repeating a color used elsewhere in the room, but usually the border is a neutral color or even white. The exact plan of the border is often best decided after the top has been finished, when you can see exactly how much more area is needed or what width border would frame the finished quilt top best.

A Starry Crown block.

Color 3

In making a quilt, color choice can really test your imagination and sense of taste. Choosing colors that you like is the best approach and certainly the simplest. Even if you are making the quilt for someone else, remember that you will be working with these colors for a long time, and it is much more pleasant to work with colors that agree with you. If you are unsure of your feel for color combinations (especially in something as large and complex as a quilt), here are some suggestions.

Choosing colors for a quilt is quite a different matter than selecting colors for clothing, new draperies, or even upholstery. Certain prints and colors that might not be appealing to you in large amounts are most attractive when used in tiny pieces in a quilt. You can be freer in your choice of bold or unusual colors, since they will be used in small amounts and in combination with other colors that will tone down or complement them. Learning to work with colors in combinations is the real trick to creating an original quilt. You should also remember that in the end the quilt is going to be very large.

If you are in doubt about combining a large number of colors, keep the number down. The fewer colors used, the easier it is to visualize the finished quilt. If too many colors are used, a confusing and perhaps even chaotic-looking quilt may be the result.

Again, careful planning is the key. This applies not only to patterns and shapes of pieces and to color in general but also to solid colors or printed fabrics and to planning a combination of both. Never buy one piece of fabric individually without comparing it with swatches of fabrics already chosen. Either shop for all the colors and prints for a particular quilt at one time or be prepared to have a large collection of various colors and prints on hand.

Solid colors can be easier to combine, yet prints do not have to be difficult. Be sure to keep in mind the size of the pieces in each block when choosing a printed fabric. Prints with large areas of pattern are rarely suitable for patchwork quilts, since a single piece will not contain the whole or enough of the print's pattern to make any sense and will look quite different when the piece is cut out and assembled into your quilt block.

A good idea in planning the colors of your quilt is to look at a color wheel and choose complementary colors. If you want a bold effect, try only primary colors or strong shades of the secondary colors. Use different shades of one basic color for a very subtle effect. Or use several different prints of the predominating color. Or combine shades or prints of one color with white for contrast.

Also in choosing your colors, the patterns you have chosen are very important. Some patterns definitely lend themselves to a certain number of colors, at least for one block. Moon over the Mountain, with only three pattern pieces, is obviously conducive to three colors per block. This quilt is generally made of repeating colors for each block, traditionally a blue print for the background square to represent the sky with a yellow solid or print for the moon and a very dark-blue solid or print for the mountain. However, each block could have three different colors or at least shades. A Windmill I block has two colors while a Windmill II generally has three colors (a light color for the top small triangle, a darker shade for the bottom small triangle, and a sharply contrasting color for the large triangle).

If you want a wider range of color or prints, choose prints that have one particular color common to all. This particular color does not have to be the predominant color of the print, but its presence will lend unity to the overall quilt.

Use solid colors for both contrast and continuity. Use white freely as contrast to make intricate patterns stand out. If you don't like white, consider beige, light gray, or other neutral shades. Black, blue, and any dark brown are very interesting neutral colors to work with, but don't overuse these darker neutrals or they will overpower the rest of the quilt. You can change the pattern of dark and light neutrals for alternate squares. Or you can have one main color for a patterned square alternating with another main color, using the reverse colors for the plain blocks.

If you are planning your quilt for a specific room, the amount of natural light in the room may influence your color choice. If the room doesn't get much light, you might want to choose warm, bright tones. If you have lots of light or live in a very warm climate, you might want to use some of the cooler shades. What are the warm colors? Red, yellow, and all the colors in between on the color wheel. They are cheery, stimulating, exciting. Cool colors range from all shades of blue up to yellow on the color wheel. These colors are intended to be calming, restful, soothing. In planning color, light and dark are important. Darker colors are more powerful and exciting, but they tend to be heavier. Pastel shades are more subtle.

Making a Sample Block

Earlier I suggested drawing your pattern and coloring it to correspond with the colors chosen for the quilt. The next step is to make a sample block of your chosen pattern and colors. In fact, you might want to try out various combinations for one pattern. Of course, you don't want to spend hours and hours making an endless array of blocks before making a choice, so it's best to use pencil and paper for most of your planning. A colored drawing or a sample block will tell you if you like your basic pattern or color combination before you go further. If you are satisfied, just remember that the larger quilt will be quite different from each individual block. This sample block will also be very useful later as a model for assembling subsequent blocks.

After you have made several blocks, lay them out on a flat surface and see how you like them together. If you are not sure you like the way they will look joined together, consider adding alternate plain blocks or lattice strips—unless you are making a hexagon, a Log Cabin, or a Lone Star quilt that cannot be separated because the pattern is always joined to another pattern.

If you decide you like the use of solid-colored alternate blocks or lattice strips, then replan the total number of blocks you will need to finish the quilt.

Size

4

Before beginning a quilt, you must estimate its finished size. The size should be figured with care, since the whole project can be ruined if a last-minute change in overall size is indicated. The whole pattern should be planned precisely, with the size of the finished quilt determining the actual size of each individual block.

We will concern ourselves here only with quilts to be used as bedcovers, since size is a minor point in making wall hangings.

To estimate size, you need answers to the following questions:

1. What is the exact size of the bed the quilt will cover? If you cannot determine the exact size, then what standard size do you wish to make the quilt?

2. Will the quilt be used as a bedspread and hang down to the floor on three sides? If yes, you must first measure the top of the mattress, then the distance from the top of the mattress to the floor. The dimensions of a standard double-bed mattress are 54 × 75, so if the bed is 22 inches high, you would estimate the finished quilt size as follows: width of mattress (54), plus distance from top of mattress to the floor (22) times 2 (44) equals a width of 98 inches. Before deciding on the length, decide if you want the quilt to cover and tuck under the pillows. If yes, allow an extra 12 inches. So the length of the mattress (75), plus the amount for pillows (12), plus the distance from top of mattress to the floor (22) equals 109 inches. This quilt will now touch the floor on three sides and cannot be made any larger. You now need to figure a workable block size for this rectangular-shaped quilt. The length is a little more flexible than the width, since you can always tuck more or less quilt under the pillows. But there is no way to use up extra quilt on the sides, so it is best to plan your quilt to be a few inches off the floor on all sides. In this case, 96 × 108 will be 1 inch off the floor all around; also, both the length and width are exactly divisible by 12 for figuring block size. If you don't want 12-inch blocks, you can change the size of the block and even out the overall quilt with a border. Some quilts have borders on only three sides—the bottom and the two sides.

If you don't want the quilt to cover and tuck under pillows, you can make pillow shams which repeat any pattern block or are a variation of your basic quilt pattern. The shams do not need to be filled and quilted. If you decide to have your quilt reach just to the top of the bed under the pillows, then figure the length of the quilt by adding the length of the mattress (54) to the height of the bed (in the above example, it was 22 inches). So 75 plus 22 equals 97, which must be rounded off to fit in with your block size. To be 1 inch off the floor on three sides and to the head of the bed on the fourth side, this quilt should measure 96 × 96.

3. If you want to use your quilt to cover only the top of the mattress and to hang over the sides only to the top of a dust ruffle, then estimate the quilt's size as follows: the width of the mattress top, plus double the distance from the mattress top to the dust ruffle equals the width of the quilt; the length of the mattress, plus one distance from mattress top to dust ruffle, plus 12 inches to cover and tuck under the pillows equals the length of the quilt. For a standard-sized double bed with a 6-inch-thick mattress, 10 inches is a good distance for overhang to top of dust ruffle. So the figures would work out as follows: 54 plus 20 equals 74 inches for the width; 75 plus 10 plus 12 equals 97 inches for the length. So the finished size should be 74 × 97 rounded off to accommodate an even number of blocks across and down (or blocks separated by a consistent width of lattice strip). Twelve-inch blocks of 6 across and 8 down would give you a quilt of 72 × 96 inches without any border. If you prefer a more generous side drop, make the quilt 84 × 96. This will give you 15 inches on each side.

4. If you want to use your quilt under a spread as a blanket, use the following facts to estimate your size: The quilt should hang down 8 to 10 inches on each side of the bed to cover one or two people without sliding off. If you want to tuck in the quilt at the bottom of the bed as you would a blanket, add about 6 inches in addition to the thickness of the mattress. If you add the length of the mattress to the above measurement, the quilt will come to the top of the bed after it is tucked under at the bottom or

give you several inches to turn back over the covers. For a double bed of 54 × 75 with a mattress of standard thickness, the finished quilt size should be between 70 and 74 inches wide and 89 inches long. Again round off these numbers to be evenly divisible by your block size.

Of course, the simplest way to measure the ideal size for your blanket-style quilt is to measure the size of the blanket already used on the bed.

A chart listing standard mattress sizes and various quilt sizes is given below for determining rough estimates. The quilt sizes have been rounded off to the nearest multiple of 12 for ease of dividing into 12-inch blocks, so be sure to figure more closely, using the above guidelines, if you plan to use other than 12-inch blocks (or if you are going to use lattice strips or borders).

Twelve inches has been used as the block size for the following chart, but it is by no means the only workable block size. If you are making a cover for a twin bed, which has a 39-inch mattress, you might prefer 13-inch blocks so that three full blocks fit exactly across the top.

Quilts used to wrap an infant in, as an afghan thrown over the back of a piece of furniture, or as a traditional lap robe are not included in the above chart because they are not meant to cover a bed. The standard size for these quilts is about 30 × 48 inches, but obviously this size is quite flexible.

If you are planning a very large quilt (for example, a standard king-sized bedspread of 120 × 108) remember that the largest sheet of batting available is 90 × 108. So if you are making a quilt larger than these dimensions, you will have to piece the batting material. Also remember that the bigger and heavier your quilt, the more difficult it is to work with at all stages of sewing, as well as in washing, dry cleaning, and storing.

BED	MATTRESS SIZE	SPREAD SIZE	COVERLET SIZE	BLANKET SIZE
King	78 × 80	120 × 108	96 × 108	108 × 96
Queen	60 × 80	96 × 108	84 × 108	84 × 96
Double	54 × 75	96 × 108	72 or 84 × 96	84 × 96
Twin	39 × 75	72 × 108	60 × 96	60 × 96
Daybed	30 × 75	72 × 108	60 × 96	60 × 96
Crib	28 × 51	Not applicable	36 × 54	36 × 54

5
Fabric

Now that you have chosen the pattern and colors for the top of your quilt, you are ready to select the fabrics. Today, fabrics are available in an endless variety of materials, both in knitted and woven forms, from cottons, woolens, and linens to Dacrons, nylons, polyesters, Banlons, etc. However, the best fabrics to use for quilting have been around for generations—woven cottons and cotton blends.

Deciding on Fabrics

Decide what kind of look you want your quilt to have, how well the fabric will cooperate through the cutting and sewing (both piecing and quilting), how the quilt will feel when it is finished, and how the quilt will be cared for.

The most suitable fabrics for making quilts have consistent textures. It is best not only for looks but also for ease in sewing, cutting, and caring for the finished product to choose fabrics of the same weight and texture. The best fabrics are 100-percent cotton; the next best, blends of cotton. Such fabrics as percales (available in solid colors as well as some prints), muslins, calicoes, and ginghams come in both 100-percent cotton and blended with polyester. If you buy a blended fabric, the higher the percentage of cotton, the better it will be for quilting. Look for lightweight fabrics in cotton or cotton blends. They should also feel both durable and soft. After all, a cover that feels rough or stiff is uncomfortable to sleep under. The weave of the fabric should be even (the same number of threads should run both across and lengthwise, and all the threads should be of the same thickness).

Stay away from fabrics that are very loosely woven (they fray, wrinkle, and tear easily) or very tightly woven. Tightly woven fabrics and those that have been treated with permanent-press or soil-release finishes are almost impossible to work with, especially if you are making a quilt by hand. It is very difficult to penetrate these materials with a needle and thread to assemble the small pieces for the top. Although there are many small and charming prints in heavy fabrics, they are bad risks for quilts. If you plan to piece the quilt on the machine, all but the most tightly woven fabrics will be suitable from a working viewpoint. But remember that you must also quilt by machine or tie or tuft the quilt; hand quilting would be impossible. If the fabric is too difficult to piece by hand, it is certainly too difficult to sew through three layers (top, batting, and backing) and sometimes three layers of top when you cross through seams in quilting.

One of the most frequently used fabrics in our grandmother's day was muslin. Today it is available in various types (100-percent cotton, cotton/polyester blends, permanent press) and in a whole range of prices. It is still relatively inexpensive compared to other fabrics, but you must be careful when buying muslin; good quality fabric is a must. Muslin is still as desirable for piecing or for use as a background, border, or backing as it was a hundred years ago. Just be sure to apply all the same quality tests to muslin as you would for other fabrics you buy. Also, *buy enough for one whole quilt at a time*. Muslin comes in both bleached (white) and unbleached (a natural buff color), and it is produced by several different textile houses. Shades of bleached or white will vary slightly from bolt to bolt, from manufacturer to manufacturer. And shades of unbleached muslin will vary even more. The quality of a fabric is determined by the number of threads per inch— the higher the number, the better the quality in general, but high quality doesn't necessarily mean ease in quilting. Be sure the weave is not too tight to sew through.

For printed fabrics, calicoes are ideal because they feature very small prints in an endless variety of colors. Like muslin, they are available in 100-percent cotton, cotton/polyester blends, and even in permanent press.

Other small prints that are good for making quilts are ginghams and plaids with small repeating patterns. Ginghams are checkered patterns made up of one color woven with white. The traditional gingham has a very small square, but it can have up to 2-inch checks. Ginghams are usually found only in cotton/polyester blends.

Small polka dots can be visually quite striking in patchwork quilts, as can stripes, but the appropriateness of stripes depends on their width and the size of your pattern pieces. Again, try to find 100-percent cotton, regardless of the print.

Some very attractive calicolike prints can be found in sailcloth or Indian head prints, which are available in 100-percent cotton. But these materials are very closely woven and comparatively heavy, and therefore, are too difficult to sew by hand.

Batiste is a very lightweight cotton fabric. It is the fabric handkerchiefs are often made from and can be used for quilts, especially if you want a very soft quilt. However, batiste is usually sheer and is not the most durable of fabric choices.

Percale is usually associated with sheets and solid colors, although it is available in prints too. It is a smooth, evenly woven cloth, available in both 100-percent cotton and cotton/polyester blends. Broadcloth is also a good-quality, medium-weight cotton or cotton blend that is available in a wide variety of colors. But both percale and broadcloth can be very tightly woven and difficult to sew through, so you should look carefully at these fabrics before you buy them to make sure they will be practical for sewing.

Keep in mind the rule of using consistent weight and textured fabrics. If you try to combine different weights and/or textures, you will discover undreamed of problems when seaming together different kinds of fabrics. An extreme example would be combining satin and corduroy; one is very smooth and slippery while the other has a thick nap that bunches as it is sewn. Also, fabrics of different weights will have puckered seams after they are stitched together.

Knitted fabrics are out of the question because they curl up at the edges after they are cut. Knits, too, have a habit of stretching. You should, in fact, avoid any fabric with even the slightest amount of stretch to it. It can throw off your entire pattern if even one edge is ever-so-slightly longer than the adjoining one. And after everything is stitched, the seams will no doubt pucker. Knits are also quite apt to shrink and stretch when washed.

Not only is it easier to work with fabrics of one kind than with combinations, but it also makes your finished quilt easier to care for. Of minor importance in choosing fabrics but still worth considering (especially if your new quilt will be washed frequently), is the factor of even wear. Fabrics of the same weight and texture tend to wear at the same rate, growing older together gracefully.

Judging Fabric Quality

Watch for the trademark *Sanforized* or the word *preshrunk* on labels. You can be sure that these fabrics will not shrink more than 2 to 3 percent.

Consider sheerness and opaqueness. Be wary of sheer fabrics, particularly those used for dress linings. Most cottons and cotton/polyester blends in prints are thick enough to be opaque. But in solid colors, it is sometimes difficult to find a whole range of colors and shades (except in dress-lining materials). A threefold problem exists with these fabrics. Seams of a darker or printed fabric, pieced in the top, will show through when the seams are pressed to one side. In piecing, you never press seams open because it puts unnecessary stress on them. When seams are pressed to one side, it is a nuisance at best and impossible at worst to be sure you have turned all darker seams inward to avoid showthrough next to a sheer fabric. Secondly, the color of the fabric, if sheer enough to see through, will quite often look different when quilted (over white batting) than you expected when you first saw the fabric on the bolt. Thirdly, sheer fabrics are more likely to fray than others.

To be certain of the quality you are buying, buy only those fabrics with a full description of contents—shrinkage allowance, washing instructions, colorfastness, etc.—printed on the bolt. Note carefully if the fabrics say "Do not dry-clean" or "Dry-clean only." You must be careful not to combine special-care fabrics.

There are many fabrics of perfect suitability for quilting that won't be marked at all. If you want to use these, just consider the following before you buy: you want fabrics of a lightweight, even texture that are machine washable and dryable. This means they must be colorfast and nonshrinkable; they should be soft to the touch yet sturdy and opaque. Look at the fabric on the bolt. You can judge most of the above characteristics by your own eye and touch. First, hold it up to the light or put it over a piece of white fabric; if you can't see through it and if the color doesn't lighten a lot, the fabric's opacity is sufficient. Next, feel the cloth. If it is soft to the touch, it will remain so. If it is not soft, why not? Perhaps because the threads are very thick or very tightly woven and therefore will be hard to work with. Or, if it is stiff because it has been treated, see if that stiffness can be washed out. The fabric should be about the same weight and texture as a shirt or blouse. Next, look at the end of the bolt. If it is stretched out of shape or the grains of the fabric look wavy, it is not a good choice for patchwork; it may stretch as you cut it or try to sew it to another piece. This may not seem very important at the outset, but remember you are likely to be working with several hundred pieces and any added difficulties with fabric are greatly multiplied by the number of pieces.

Also be wary of fabrics with the design printed on. If the design is not even with the grain of the cloth, you can go crazy trying to cut out the fabric on the grain line while having the pattern repeat itself exactly, although the latter factor is not always important. Such fabric can be used, but must be straightened along the grain line before cutting and may not be worth the extra trouble of straightening.

See if the ends will fray. Take the cut end of the bolt between your thumb and forefinger and rub it. You don't really have to beat the fabric into a rag to be sure, but it is a good test of fraying potential. You can imagine the disaster you would have trying to sew together tiny pieces of fabric all ravelling at the edges, to say nothing of a finished quilt that comes apart at the seams the first time it is washed. Pull the fabric slightly along the grain. Does it stretch as you pull? If yes, then you don't want the fabric. Does it become a mass of wrinkles if you wad a handful in your fist for a couple of seconds? If it does, you don't want it because your quilt should never be ironed. Just remember that you don't want something that will always look wilted in your finished quilt.

As for shrinkage and colorfastness, you can test at home because all fabrics must be prewashed and ironed before cutting and sewing.

6
Estimating Amounts of Fabric

You have chosen your pattern and your color scheme, and you have probably made up a sample block or two. The next step toward making your quilt is to estimate how much fabric of each color and shape you need.

Using Your Sample

If you have made a sample block, take a good long look at it. How long did it take you to assemble it? Now figure the size of the top of your quilt. How much of that will be patterned blocks? See how many of your finished sample blocks will be needed to make the top of your quilt the desired size. You can tailor the size of the block to the size of the quilt, if you like, or you can adapt the size of the top to accommodate an even number of blocks of desired size. The latter is the simpler method.

For instance, you may want a quilt to be 90 × 108 inches. This is a good standard size, which can accommodate double or queen-sized mattresses as coverlets or blankets. If you use 9-inch blocks, you will need 10 across and 12 down, and no size adjustments are necessary. If you increase the block size to 12 inches, you will have 7½ across and 9 down. Therefore, you need to change the top size either to 84 × 108 (7 blocks by 9 blocks) for a double (decreasing 3 inches per side) or to 96 × 108 (8 blocks and 9 blocks) for a queen size (increasing 3 inches per side). If you want 15-inch blocks, you would have 6 across and 7^1/$_5$ down, which means adjusting the length to 105 inches so that you can have an even number of blocks for length. For 18-inch blocks, you would have 5 across and 6 down. From these examples, you can see that both the size of the block and the overall dimensions of the quilt are quite flexible; it's merely a matter of finding the block dimension that can be evenly divided into both the width and length of the top.

Of course, you can also adjust the size of the top by joining the patterned blocks with lattice strips of various widths or by adding one or more borders of whatever width you like. Remember that a quilt made up of 8 blocks across and 9 down (96 × 108 with 12-inch blocks) has a total of 72 blocks, and if all of those are patterned, you have the length of time you spent to assemble the sample multiplied by 72. If you make the same size quilt all in patterned blocks of 18 inches, you will need only 30 blocks and it will take considerably less time.

To increase the block size from 12 to 18 inches, you need some basic math. Say your block is made up of a Four Patch variation, like Windmill I with two triangles making a 6 × 6 square. Four of these squares are joined to make a 12-inch block. If you want to enlarge your patterned block to 15 inches, make each of those 4 squares 7½ × 7½, or for an 18-inch block, 9 × 9. Then adjust the size of the triangles accordingly. Measure all the sizes of the new triangles and make a new pattern. Or if you are doing an Irish Chain, of which one block of the pattern is made up of 5 little squares by 5 little squares of 2 inches each, you will have a 10-inch block. Increase your little squares from 2 × 2 to 3 × 3 or 4 × 4 for either a 15-inch square or a 20-inch square. These are simple patterns to readjust, but you can readjust even more complicated ones. For instance, a Log Cabin square of a common width of rectangle and center square of 2 inches makes a 14-inch square. If reduced to a 1-inch width it makes a 7-inch square; if that width is increased to 3 inches, it makes a 21-inch square if you use the traditional 13-piece block. However, in Log Cabin, you can vary the size of the block by adding or subtracting the number of logs used to make up a block. For instance,

take your 2-inch square for the center. If you add 12 logs as is the usual amount, you build a 14-inch block. If you add 4 more logs of 2-inch widths, you will have an 18-inch block. The trick, however, is that you must add or subtract logs in multiples of 4 in order to keep the block square, which is important to maintain consistent overall patterns when joining the blocks. Remember to refigure the total number of pieces in the quilt when you adjust your block size so that you are conscious of how long or how complicated you are making your project in terms of time.

Obviously, one shortcut is to increase the size of the pieces within the block to enlarge the block itself rather than adding more pieces to the block. But remember that increasing the size of the pieces alters the visual effect of the finished quilt. To what extent the effect is changed depends on the total number of pieces in the block. For example, compare a simple Windmill I of 8 triangles, enlarged from a 6-inch block to a 12-inch and to an 18-inch block, with an Irish Chain of 25 squares, enlarged from a 5-inch square to a 10-inch and to a 15-inch square. Both block sizes are doubled and then tripled, and the dimensions of each piece are doubled and tripled. The Windmill I triangle increases from 3 inches per short side to 6 inches and then 9 inches per short side,

Four blocks of a triple Irish Chain.

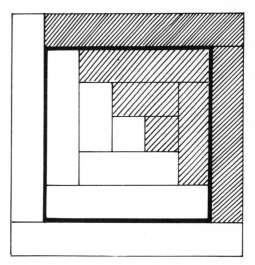

A traditional Log Cabin block of 13 rectangles or logs can be increased in overall size by adding 4 more rectangles.

while the Irish Chain square increases from 1 inch per side to 2 and 3 inches. If you draw these two patterns to scale, you will see that the change in the Irish Chain doesn't seem as great as the change in the Windmill. This difference in effect is heightened in the finished quilt.

Estimating the Top

By now you should know how many patterned blocks you need. Let's say you are going to make a Windmill I pattern for a double bed. You are going to alternate 12-inch patterned blocks with solid-colored blocks and add a 6-inch solid border all around. The finished dimensions will be 96 × 108. It is a good idea to have an odd rather than an even number of blocks across and down for a balanced look when alternating patterned and solid blocks. If this is not feasible, at least try for an odd number across. Adjust the block size or quilt top size. For example, if you plan a patterned top of 84 × 96, you will have 7 blocks across and 8 down, which means a total of 56 blocks, 28 of which are patterned and 28 of which are plain. You need 8 triangles of two different colors for each patterned block (a total of 224 triangles—112 of Color A and 112 of Color B). You need to add ½ inch for seam allowance for each piece (¼ inch for each side).

Figure the triangles as though they were half squares. Each triangle will measure 6 inches per short side. So if you position 2 triangles (with a ¼-inch seam allowance between them) to make a square, you need a piece of fabric 6¾ × 6¾. This is estimating to get the absolute most out of a piece of fabric, and it is also the simplest mathematical formula. Remember, you must line up right angles on the grain line of fabric. If you lay out your pattern pieces carefully with just ½ inch between each triangle from lengthwise edge to edge, you can cut 12 triangles from one row of a 45-inch width of fabric, after subtracting the selvages. You need 112 pieces, and if you allow 7 inches for depth (rounded off to the next highest whole number from 6¾ to simplify) in rows of 12 triangles across, you need 10 rows 7 inches deep, which means 2 yards of fabric.

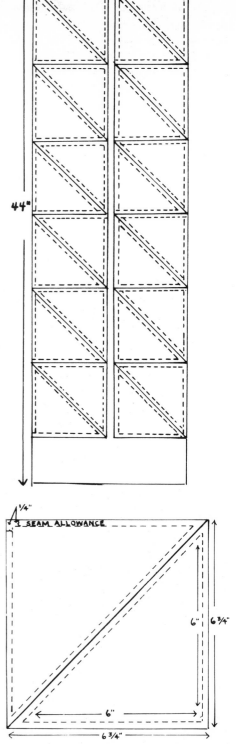

To lay out triangles for cutting with minimum waste, place each short side on lengthwise grain of fabric allowing only the seam allowance of ¼ inch of each side.

You will have to measure and cut very carefully to get all 112 pieces out, so you may want to allow more than 2 yards of Color A and 2 yards of Color B.

For the alternating plain squares, you need squares 12½ × 12½. This includes ¼ inch on each side for seam allowance. You should cut carefully between squares. If you are at all uneasy about precision, space your squares 1 or more inches apart. In this instance, in 45-inch-wide fabric, you can cut only three 12½-inch squares across, whether you space them ½ inch apart or 3 inches apart. You need 28 squares. If you cut 3 per row, you need 10 rows at least 12½ inches deep, which would be 3½ yards. (When estimating, always round off to the higher ¼ yard.)

For your border, you can estimate two ways. If you don't mind piecing the lengths, you will need less fabric. Your finished length is 108 inches, which is your finished border length. For a 6-inch border cut from 45-inch fabric, subtract 1 inch for selvages, so use 44 inches for the fabric width when estimating. You will need three 7-inch widths to make a border strip 109 inches long (108 inches for the finished border plus ½-inch seam allowance on each end). It is better to allow ½ inch for seam allowance on the sides for borders, although if you prefer to use ¼ inch as for piecing, it is sufficient. You will have two seams in each border length, so cut 3 strips 7 inches wide in equal lengths of 37 inches for each long border. This is six 37-inch strips for both long sides of the quilt. Allow 1 more inch for cutting room (8 inches). Be sure to cut the lengths for the border strips on the grain of the fabric, or you may have some strange stretching in your finished quilt. After adding ½ inch to each side of the 6-inch border plus 1 more inch for cutting, you have 8-inch widths. You then need another 6 widths of 8 inches each to piece the border for the top and bottom of the quilt. The finished top will measure 96 inches across, therefore from 44 inches of fabric, you need 6 equal pieces of 33 inches long, allowing for ½-inch seam allowance on each end. The borders for the top and bottom can be pieced out of 5 widths if you wish, but you will have either more seams or unequal distances between the

seams. This all adds up to 8-inch widths multiplied by 12 (3 strips for each side of the quilt) or 2¾ yards of fabric for the borders. If you don't want to go to all the trouble of figuring and cutting and piecing for the borders, you can simply figure the longest piece you will need for a border, which for the example we are using, is 109 (108 finished length plus ½-inch seam allowance on each end or 3¼ yards of fabric). The 2 shorter 97-inch lengths will fit side by side with the 2 longer ones, allowing 7 inches for each width (6 finished width plus seam allowance), plus 3 inches between strips for cutting, for a total of 31 inches across. This is only ½ yard more than you needed for pieced borders.

If you want to use the same fabric for the border as you have for the alternate plain blocks, you can combine your estimates to save yourself from buying extra fabric. This is how it works out. You have 2 long strips 7 × 109 inches for a total of 14 × 109; then allow 1 inch in between for cutting room plus 2 strips 7 × 97 (total of 14 × 97) with another 2 inches for cutting or 31 inches wide for borders. You have 44 inches (the width of the fabric minus the selvages) minus 31 for borders and cutting, leaving 13 inches of fabric. You need 12½ inches across for each square. This leaves you ½ inch cutting room between border and square, so you must cut carefully. You can cut a row of squares to allow for 109 inches for a long border. You have 3¼ yards or 117 inches of fabric out of this strip. In 117 inches you can cut 9 squares (allowing 12½ inches for each square) from that strip. You can cut one more below the two short 97-inch border strips. This gives you 10 squares; you need 28 in all. In cutting the original rows of squares from 45-inch fabric, you could cut 3 across, so you now need enough fabric for 6 rows 12½ inches wide, or 75 inches, which when converted to the higher ¼ yard is 2¼ yards. You needed 3¼ yards to cut unpieced borders, and if you add another 2¼ for squares, you need a total of 5½ yards for both the solid blocks and the 6-inch border. If you buy separately, you need 3¼ yards for borders (2¾ yards if you piece) and 4 yards for the squares.

The estimates for the plain 12-inch blocks

and for the 6-inch border remain the same for any quilt pattern you make that is 96 × 108 with 12-inch blocks. The amount of fabric needed for the patterned blocks varies, depending on the number, sizes, and colors of the pieces in the pattern.

If you want to make this same 96 × 108 quilt with 18-inch blocks, you have to increase the dimensions to 102 × 120 with a border. Or if you forget the border, you'll have five 18-inch blocks across the top and six blocks down for a 90 × 108 size, which is close to the original size.

To figure fabric for Windmill I, you need 30 blocks, 15 patterned and 15 plain. For 15 patterned blocks of 8 triangles, you need 120 triangles, 60 of Color A and 60 of Color B.

When enlarged to 18-inch blocks, your new triangle is 9 inches per short side. So when made into squares of 2 triangles for cutting, the squares are 9¾ inches (including seam allowances). With 45-inch fabric, you can cut 8 triangles per row. This means you need 8 rows 10 inches deep or 2¼ yards of both Color A and Color B. (Note: you needed 2 yards of each color for the 12-inch blocks in this pattern.) For the plain blocks, you can only cut 2 across. You need 15 blocks 18½ inches square, which means you need enough fabric for 8 rows 18½ inches deep, or 4¼ yards. For the same quilt in 12-inch blocks you needed only 3½ yards. From these comparisons, you can see that increasing the size of the pieces within the block itself doesn't appreciably increase total fabric amounts for smaller pieces, but it does greatly increase fabric amounts when increasing the larger plain squares.

Now let's figure the same 96 × 108 quilt using 36-inch fabric with the original 12-inch block size and with the 6-inch border. You need 112 triangles of Color A and 112 triangles of Color B, and you need 6¾ inches per 2 triangles. That means you can cut 10 triangles per row. You need 12 rows, 7 inches deep, which is 2½ yards. (Note: this is ½ yard more for the same number of same sized triangles in 45-inch fabric.)

The difference in yardage for the plain squares is even greater, because you can cut only two 12½-inch squares per row. You need 28 squares, which means 14 rows 12½ inches deep, or 5 yards. In the first example, you needed 3½ yards for the plain squares.

For an unpieced border, you need the same amount as for the first example, 3¼ yards, because the needed widths fit across the 36-inch fabric. There is no reason to piece this pattern, since the narrower fabric requires the same amount of yardage (you need 4 strips to piece each long border instead of 3). Neither do you save fabric by using the same color for the plain squares and the border, because there is no extra area after cutting border strips to cut squares as in the first example.

7
Making Patterns

For patchwork, there are certain standard shapes. The most common and frequently used are squares, triangles, rectangles, diamonds, hexagons, and octagons. Plus, most patchwork patterns are combinations of shapes that form a square when put together.

By now you have no doubt decided on your basic pattern, the size of your finished quilt, and the size of the individual blocks. But before you begin cutting and sewing together your top, you need cutting patterns to work from. You can either buy or make a master pattern piece, called a template, from which you can either cut all of your pieces or make additional patterns for cutting. You need a template for each shape and size you are going to use.

Templates are made from very sturdy materials, such as tin or some other metal, plastic, linoleum, or even wood. The template must always have exact edges and corners or angles. If more than 1 piece is used per size, it must be the exact replica of every other piece in that size and shape. If the master pattern piece frays or wears at the edges or angles, even slightly, before you have finished cutting out all the pieces you need, you will not have pieces of fabric exactly cut, which will mean that your pattern will not fit together correctly. The preciseness of the pieces is vital in patchwork, so do not use shortcuts when making your patterns or cutting your fabric.

If you have large pieces making up large blocks, you obviously do not have to use the pattern as frequently as you would with tiny pieces. However, be sure to have accurate patterns even for the largest of pieces.

Templates made of metal and plastic can be purchased from some quilt supply stores and mail-order houses that specialize in quilting supplies. (See Sources of Supply.) These templates are usually found in small sizes from 1 to 2 or sometimes 3 inches for length of side. Be sure to buy only those templates which have been die-cut. Most have textured surfaces to reduce the possibility of the pattern slipping on either fabric or cardboard while the template is being traced around.

You can also buy precut cardboard or heavy paper templates, which can be pinned to the fabric and cut around. Just be sure to purchase enough cardboard pieces to hold up through all your cutting. (About 50 pieces is the maximum number from one cardboard template before the piece starts to wear.)

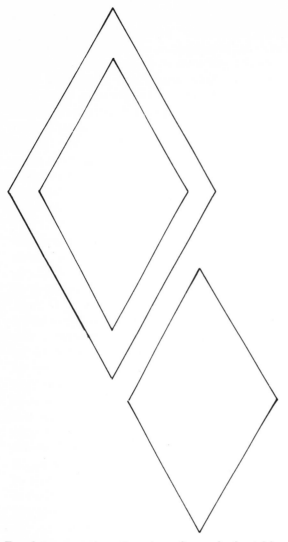

Templates are master pattern pieces often made of metal for sturdiness. Window templates are useful for marking seam allowances.

The cost of these templates is nominal, considering it might take you hours to make an accurate master pattern. The most expensive metal template, if purchased singly, would be under two dollars; a metal template with window would be under three dollars; and most sets of 3 to 6 pieces could be purchased for between $2.50 and $5.00. These templates are well worth the price.

Making Your Own Template

If you are making a pattern in sizes for which ready-made templates are not available, or if you decide to make your own, here are some suggestions.

You can make your master template or make other pieces from the master out of heavy cardboard, sandpaper, or linoleum. Sandpaper is a good material, because when placed rough-side down on fabric, it can be held or pinned and either traced or cut around without slipping on the fabric. However, be especially careful not to cut into the template. You can cut a new piece of fabric, but you can't repair the template without danger of losing its exact shape. Sandpaper and cardboard both wear around the edges with continued handling. They are good materials, however, to use with large-sized patterns, like the Windmill. If you are making 58 blocks, you will have to use that same template 464 times. You can make a master template and then make a dozen or more pattern pieces from that template to use for your actual cutting.

To ensure exact right angles for squares or right triangles, buy a draftsman's right-angle triangle. These triangles come in a variety of sizes in both metal and plastic, and they can be purchased in graphic art supply stores. Most of them are cut out in the center (usually rounded) for convenient handling. If you want to use both the inside and outside edges, be sure to select one with the inside corners trued.

If you are making your own pattern, first draw it exactly on a piece of graph paper. You can then glue the graph paper to cardboard or sandpaper and cut out the piece very carefully. If you have penciled lines, always cut slowly

There are also window templates available in standard small sizes with ¼-inch borders that allow you to mark both the cutting line and the seam line.

I strongly advise purchasing templates for particularly small pieces or for more difficult shapes (diamonds and hexagons, for example). Even triangles can be difficult to make exactly. Combination packages—made up of a square, a triangle, and a diamond or of a combination of various sizes and shapes—can be purchased. All are made to scale, and various combinations of patterns can be made with one kit.

along the outside edge of the line. The thinner the line you have drawn, the easier and more exact your cutting will be. Also, when tracing around a template, be sure to hold your pencil at the same angle on all sides to ensure drawing your line as close to the edge of the template as possible. This all sounds very time-consuming and perhaps too cautious, but you can't be too careful in making your patterns and cutting your pieces exactly.

If you don't want to bother with the mess of gluing graph paper to cardboard or sandpaper, you can transfer the design to the cardboard or sandpaper with carbon paper. Place the carbon paper between the graph paper and the sandpaper and redraw your pattern piece. When drawing or tracing a straight-sided pattern piece, use a straightedge. Or you can use a tracing wheel, which pricks tiny holes through the graph paper; the impression made on the cardboard or sandpaper can then be drawn over or dusted with chalk or powder, or if the impression is clear enough, it can be cut along as is.

Enlarging Your Patterns

Take a piece of graph paper and trace the original pattern or piece on it, lining up the corners and angles with the lines on the graph paper. Then take another piece of graph paper and redraw your pattern to the desired size, square by square. You can then transfer the pattern from the graph paper to a heavier material as described previously. You can make patterns for appliqués, which have no straight edges or exact corners, the same way. Trace the picture or shape onto graph paper, and then enlarge or reduce it by drawing square to square on the graph paper. If your pattern will be repeated several times, you should then transfer your drawing to heavier paper, cardboard, or sandpaper, following the suggestions given earlier. If you are drawing a freehand appliqué pattern, you can use any kind of heavy paper or even cardboard to make your pattern.

Appliqué patterns can be drawn onto a material called Pellon, a nonwoven fabric which can be ironed onto another fabric. Pellon is often used as a stiffening fabric in collars or as an interlining in belts, waistbands, or facings. Pellon can be cut to size, ironed onto the fabric to be cut, and then cut around allowing ¼ inch by eye for turning under the piece to be appliquéd. This does stiffen and ever so slightly thicken the appliquéd piece, but that can be a desirable quality unless you plan to quilt through the appliqué. If you plan to quilt around the appliquéd pieces, which is a common quilting method, the Pellon will accent the raised effect achieved by the quilting. It certainly makes cutting patterned pieces of fabric simpler than the traditional method of tracing around a pattern and then cutting and then turning under seam allowances.

8
Preparing and Cutting the Fabric

Preparing your fabric before you begin cutting or sewing is very important. If you are using all washable fabrics, remember to machine wash and dry and to iron before going further. If for any reason, you don't think a fabric will respond well to such treatment, then you had better not use it in a quilt that will be washed. This is also the time to test the fabric for shrinkage and colorfastness. If in doubt as to a fabric's shrinkability, or to be on the safe side for any fabric, measure the piece of fabric before you wash, dry, and iron it; then remeasure it afterward. If the difference is great, it is a good idea to repeat the measuring, washing, and drying to make sure it won't shrink anymore. Most cottons shrink 2 to 3 percent when washed for the first time, but usually they will not shrink further. Blends usually shrink less than 100-percent cottons, and they shrink only during the first wash.

If prewashing seems like an unnecessary step, and you are thinking of skipping it, think for a minute what your finished quilt, which you spent so much time and effort making, will look like if one of the pieces of fabric shrinks and pulls the pattern all out of shape. Those triangles in brilliant blue with puckered seams can be a very sad sight.

The same is true for testing for colorfastness. If you think a fabric is at all likely to fade and run into other colors in the quilt, then wash it by hand in medium-hot water. If the wash or rinse water turns color, the fabric is bleeding. That doesn't mean it will bleed onto other fabrics, but it might. If it doesn't run in the first washing, it won't later; but if it does, you might try setting the dye by soaking for a short time in cool water, to which a little vinegar or salt has been added. Then wash again to make sure the setting process worked. If it didn't, reconsider using the fabric. If there's only a faint coloring in the water, don't worry. The fabric color may get lighter when washed, but it probably won't hurt other fabrics.

Bright reds are the most dangerous colors in terms of bleeding onto other colored fabrics. If you are using wools, wash them either by hand or by machine, depending on how the fabric looks to you and on the instructions for care, if any, that come with the bolt. Use cool water and Woolite or some soap especially made for washing woolens. Let the fabric dry completely. If you can't wash the wool fabrics, at least steam press the wool very carefully so that any shrinking will occur now instead of after it is made into a quilt.

If you are using scraps from old clothes or whatever, you don't need to wash them first, but if you are using scraps of fabric left over from dressmaking projects and they have not previously been washed, do wash them now. If the scraps are very small, I suggest you do them by hand.

I repeat: *all prewashing* is a precautionary measure that is well worth taking.

The finished quilt should never be ironed, but you should iron the fabrics so they will lay flat and be smooth for cutting. If any of the fabrics you have washed come out extremely wrinkled, remember that is how it will look in the quilt after it has been washed. Of course, if you are using small patterned pieces and quilt in rows that are close together, this will reduce the wrinkled look.

Washing can have another advantage. If your fabrics are at all stiff or if they have been treated to make them permanent press, or even if they are just heavier cottons, washing in hot sudsy water often helps soften them up so that they are easier to work with.

Cutting the Fabric

Now that you have prepared your fabric and assembled your pattern pieces, you are ready to lay out the patterns and cut the fabric.

It is usually more accurate to cut all the pieces you plan to use for the whole quilt at one time. Start with one color and fabric and shape. Lay out the patterns and cut all of the first size of that color. Then cut the next size and shape of that fabric, and so on until you have cut all the pieces you need from that cloth. For patchwork, always lay out the pattern pieces on the wrong side of the fabric so that any marking you do won't show on the finished block. For appliqué, however, you are cutting out pieces that will be assembled into blocks or the quilt top as a whole. By appliquéing the pieces and stitching on the right side of the block, you can lay out the patterns on the right side of the fabric and mark that side, since you will be turning under the seam allowance.

Keep separate stacks of sizes, shapes, and colors as you proceed. You may want to have several boxes to put the pieces in if they are likely to be disturbed before you finish your cutting. If you are not careful to keep all your pieces organized, you can spend many frustrating hours assembling your quilt blocks.

If you are making a scrap quilt and each block is a different combination of fabrics and colors, then it isn't necessary to do all the cutting at once. You can cut however much is easiest to work on at one sitting. For instance, if you are making a hexagonal pattern, you can cut enough to work on until you want to set up a table with pins and what-have-you for cutting. It can also be easier when doing a scrap quilt to cut fabric for one block at a time. You don't have to organize so many pieces at once. However, if you plan to repeat the colors and fabrics in more than one block, then you should cut out all those pieces at the same time.

Always cut only one piece at a time from one thickness of cloth. If you try to cut from more than one thickness, you will greatly impair the exactness you need. Take special care when cutting around corners to make them exact. If they aren't, you will have a difficult time matching edges and corners to form your pattern.

If you are using individual pattern pieces of heavy paper that can be pinned in place, cut all the pattern pieces you need for a given color and shape before you start. If that is too many to be practical, at least have enough pattern pieces or templates to cut one complete row of fabric. It takes a long time to line up all the pattern pieces on the grain of the fabric, so it is easier to cut one whole row. Again, be sure to cut all the pattern pieces from heavy enough paper or cardboard so that they can be used often without wearing out at the edges. And be sure that all the pieces are exactly the same.

Finding the Grain of the Fabric

The lengthwise grain of the fabric runs parallel to the selvages of the cloth, and the crosswise grain should intersect the lengthwise grain at an exact right angle. The bias is the diagonal line between the crosswise and lengthwise grains. If the grain lines are

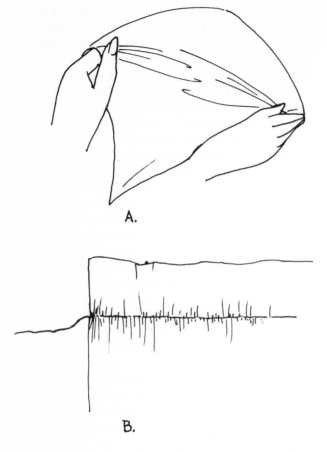

A.

B.

Straightening the grain of a fabric can be done one of two ways: either by pulling on the bias or by pulling a thread.

The selvages should be trimmed off before cutting, or at least, they should not be included in any of the cut pieces or their seam allowances. This is because the selvages would pucker where they are crossed by or join in seams. Selvages are also very difficult to sew through by hand when piecing or quilting, because they are heavier and denser than the rest of the fabric.

Locating the grain line is important because all your pieces should be cut on the grain to prevent the edges from stretching out of shape as you sew them together. Cutting the individual pieces on the grain may also prevent distortion of the pattern when washing the finished quilt.

Marking the Fabric

If you are not using individual paper patterns, but want to trace around your templates directly onto the cloth, be careful not to mark the cloth permanently. Even if you are marking on the wrong side of the fabric, as in patchwork, the lines might show through if the fabric is a light color. Don't mark with pencil because the graphite doesn't always wash out. Instead, try soft chalk, which comes in several colors and is even available in pencil form. There are disadvantages to chalk, however. It can make too wide a mark to cut along evenly, and it sometimes smears or rubs off before you have stitched together the pieces. Some felt-tip pens will mark easily without too much pressure, which can pull the cloth out of shape while a template is being traced around. But not all felt-tip pens will wash out, so read the label before using one. It may also be some time before you wash the quilt, and you may have to live with the felt-tip marks. Unless, of course, you want to wash out the colored markings after you have pieced the blocks. I find this to be an annoying additional step that can be avoided by using chalk. The best marking method depends on the size of your pieces and their shapes.

A good method for placing most shaped pieces for cutting is to pin a paper pattern, cut to the finished size of the piece, to the cloth. Then cut out the piece, leaving a ¼-inch seam allowance on all sides. If you have had some

not straight, or if your fabric has not been cut evenly at the ends, you should square it before cutting. The easiest way is to pull the fabric on the bias. If stretching on the bias doesn't straighten the grain, then you will have to find the straight by pulling a thread lengthwise, and if possible, by pulling a thread crosswise as well. At the cut end, take one of the threads and carefully separate it from the others, pull it so that it makes a slightly puckered line down the length of the fabric. This line is the grain line, or straight, of the cloth. Line your templates up parallel to this line for the lengthwise grain and perpendicular to it for the crosswise grain. On some fabrics, you can pull a crosswise thread by cutting off the selvage and pulling a loose thread crossways.

experience working with and cutting fabric and feel fairly confident about judging ¼ inch by eye, there may be no need to mark the fabric further. Certain shapes like hexagons and irregular shapes such as those used in appliqué do not have to be marked. After the piece is cut out, press under the seam allowance before removing the pattern piece. The crease is your seam line. If the seam line is clearly marked, the cutting line does not have to be as exact as when you cut a piece including seam allowance and then measure *in* ¼ inch to the seam line. But if you do want to mark the fabric, use a straightedge and measure ¼ inch all around.

Some shapes—for instance, diamonds and hexagons—must be the most carefully matched of all at the corners, especially when making star patterns out of the diamond shapes. These pieces should be marked, but it may be even better to leave the pattern pieces in place until the pieces are sewn together. Follow the preceding steps for cutting out an individual piece and pressing under the seam allowance. Then baste the seam allowance down, leaving the patterns in place. Seam together two rows of pieces, but be careful not to sew through the paper patterns. After the second row is finished, you can remove the pattern pieces from the first row. If your quilt pattern lends itself to this method, you won't be able to cut all your pieces at once unless you have a very large supply of paper patterns.

If your pieces are large enough to be sewn by machine, you can use the sole plate under the needle to gauge your seam allowance. For such pieces, be sure to cut the outside edge exactly; in this instance, don't try to cut the seam allowance by eye. Window templates, described earlier, are helpful for marking exact seam allowances.

Cutting on the Grain

The basic shape of your pattern determines how you should place it on the fabric. Fabric pulled from corner to corner (or on the bias) stretches in that direction, but not when pulled on the grain lines. Keep this in mind when placing your patterns.

Squares. Place squares so that a right angle of one of the corners corresponds to the intersection of the lengthwise and crosswise grains.

Triangles. Triangles can be cut in any of several ways. In some patterns, it is best to place the long side on the grain to minimize the stretch of that side after it is cut and sewn. In some cases, it is better to put the right angle on the intersection of crosswise and lengthwise grains so that the two short sides will not stretch; of course, this means the long side is on the bias. Another way is to draw a line from the top angle down to the center of the line opposite the top. This line is then placed on the grain.

Diamonds. Place diamonds so that the parallel sides are on the grain.

Hexagons. Place hexagons with one of the sides on the straight. This also applies to other multisided shapes. But if any multisided piece has a long side, place that side on the grain.

Curved Edges and Irregular Shapes. For cutting curved edges and irregular shapes, you have to follow a combination of the above principles and experiment with the layout of patterns on fabrics to see which way the fabric stretches the least. A good rule of thumb is to have the grain of the cut piece correspond to the grain of the underneath fabric.

Seam Allowances

When positioning the pattern on the fabric, place the pieces at least ½ inch apart to allow ¼ inch on each edge for seam allowance. You can allow as much or as little as you like for seam allowances, but I would never recommend less than ¼ inch. Many people use ⅜ inch because they feel more secure with a little more margin in case of error. I use ¼ inch simply because it makes it easier to estimate fabric. Less than ¼ inch is very tiny, and with a minimal amount of stress or fraying, the seam can pull out. Too wide a seam allowance can make for unnecessary extra fabric, which in turn, can make quilting by hand across seams troublesome.

For curved edges in both patchwork and appliqué, a narrow seam allowance is easier to turn under since curves are difficult to sew. If you are turning curves, you will need to clip to the seam line on the inner side of the curve to prevent too much bulk and pulling. If you are clipping the outside of a curve, notch it at regular intervals. How close together to make your clips or notches depends on how tight the curve is. The more gentle the curve, the easier it is to work with. In other words, the outside edge of a 6-inch circle needs infrequent clipping while a 1-inch circle is very tricky to turn under.

Organizing the Pieces

When you have finished cutting all the shapes, sizes, and colors you need to complete your quilt top, there are two ways of organizing and storing these pieces while you are working.

Earlier I discussed making a sample block so that you have a model to follow when assembling the rest of the blocks. If you are using different colors for the other blocks, you still need a model to show how all the shapes will fit together when assembled.

You can take a needle and thread and string together all the pieces of one type. Knot one end of the thread and put needle and thread through the stack of pieces, leaving a long piece of thread at the open end. For instance, if you are doing Windmill II, which has two sizes of triangles (the larger triangles of Color A and the two smaller triangles of Colors B and C), you can string the triangles of Color A on one thread, Color B on another thread, and Color C on a third. Then you can take off the pieces as you need them.

A second method is to assemble all the pieces necessary to complete one block together in the same manner. For Windmill II, that would mean 4 triangles of each color per thread.

If you are using different colors for different blocks, it is probably better to use the second method. If you are doing a Log Cabin with repeating colors, you can use either method. If you have a 13-piece block and are alternating light and dark colors, you will have 13 different stacks of fabric organized by size and color. If you organize stacks by block, you will have the same number of stacks as you have blocks in the quilt. I find it easier to use the block-stacking method of organization, because I like to work on a block at a time while watching television or even just sitting down for a few minutes.

I have a friend who made a scrap hexagon quilt of flower hexagon rings (Grandmother's Flower Garden), which has 1,406 pieces for the flowers alone. She could make 2 or 3 flowers in an evening, so she cut out enough hexagons for those 2 or 3 flowers, each of which had 3 rings of hexagons plus 1 in the center, or 37 hexagons per flower. The patterns were basted inside each piece until the rings were joined. Then the basting stitches were clipped and the pattern removed to be used again. Since each ring was a different color, the logical method of sorting the pieces was by block, which in this case was made of 3 rings of hexagons. Making the 38 flowers was the easy part. The time-consuming and exhausting part of this quilt was in setting together the rings of hexagons with white hexagons to join the blocks and fill in the spaces. More than a thousand white hexagons were needed to complete the project.

9
Assembling a Block

Patchwork Block

Lay out all the pieces that you need to make 1 block. Examine your pattern to locate the basic block. Many quilt blocks are made up of either 4 squares or 9 squares within the larger main block. If your pattern is one of these variations of a Four Patch or Nine Patch, then start by assembling the pieces for one of the squares within the larger square that is the block. Windmill I and II are Four Patch variations, as is Dutchman's Puzzle.

If you were assembling Windmill II, you would first join the two small triangles to form one large triangle, taking care that the lighter of the two small triangles is on top. Then you would join the long side of the new large triangle to the long side of the large triangle to form a square that is one-fourth of the whole block. Make sure you follow the proper color pattern and sequence for the whole block.

If you were doing Dutchman's Puzzle, you would first join two small triangles, which are usually the lightest in color, to the sides of one of the larger triangles by attaching the long side of the little triangle to one of the larger triangles. After both of the small triangles were attached to the large one, you would have a rectangle. Then you would make another rectangle by attaching two small triangles to the large triangle of the third color. When that is done, the two rectangles would be sewn together, usually with the darker triangle on the bottom, flat side down. All four squares would be made like this and then joined to one another as illustrated on page 38.

To make your block construction more logical, decide if the block can be broken into smaller or repeating units. It is usually best to build from the smallest pieces up to the larger ones. This is especially true if you are using a lot of little triangles, which are usually joined into squares or larger triangles that are then joined to other squares.

Always keep a sample block (or at least a color-keyed drawing) in front of you to make sure you have the units correctly positioned and arranged according to color. Even if you are making each block from a different combination of colors and prints, the arrangement of lights and darks, of size and shape will follow the same pattern in each block.

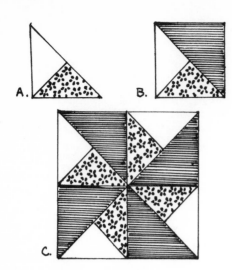

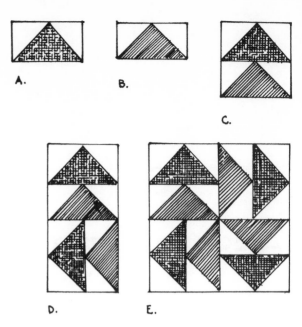

Assembling a block of Windmill II. 1. Join 2 small triangles A and B along short sides. The lighter color should be on top. 2. Join the new large triangle to triangle C along long sides. 3. After 4 squares of A, B, and C are made, position as shown and stitch together to complete the block.

Assembling a block of Dutchman's Puzzle. 1. Join two A triangles to either side of a B triangle. Attach the long side of A to a short side of B to form a rectangle. 2. Repeat the procedure to join two A triangles to either side of a C triangle to form another rectangle. 3. Seam together the two rectangles to make a square as shown with the ABA combination on top with the point of B pointing up. The ACA combination is on the bottom with C pointing up. 4. Complete two more rectangles and stitch together as above. Then join the two squares, positioned as shown. The top square has B and C points up and the bottom square has B and C pointing left. 5. Two more squares are completed of ABA and ACA combinations as before, and stitched together with B and C triangles pointing down on the top and to the right on the bottom. Then right and left sides are sewn together to complete the block.

Some blocks cannot be broken down into groups of 4 or 9 squares, and so they will have to be built up from smaller units to larger units in another way. Log Cabin and hexagon rings, as well as many of the star patterns, are built from the center outward. In Log Cabin, the center of the block is the smallest unit. In a hexagon pattern, all the units are the same size and the pattern is worked from the center out.

Whatever the arrangement of the block, the best way to assemble it will reveal itself if you examine the block carefully and simply do what seems logical.

Sewing the Units Together

Before you actually sew together the small pieces that make up your block, pin or baste them together. Be very careful to match the edges exactly at corners, angles, or points. Also take care not to stretch any of the pieces while you are pinning, basting, or sewing. Pinning is usually sufficient with no need for basting unless the pattern piece is very large or irregularly shaped and might slip. If you are sewing by machine, make sure the pins are placed at right angles to the seam line so that they won't

catch on the pressure foot or cause an uneven row of stitching. For some very large patchwork designs sewn on the machine, basting makes it more certain that the corners are perfectly matched.

You can sew the pieces either by hand or by machine, whichever is easier for you. If you haven't done much machine sewing, it may be just as fast, and more precisely done the first time around, to sew by hand. For blocks made up of very small units, hand sewing is the most precise way to assemble the block. To line up small units and to end your row of stitches exactly ¼ inch from the edge of the fabric is extremely difficult if not downright impossible on the machine. And hand sewing has the added advantage of being transportable.

If on the other hand, your pattern lends itself easily and technically to being done on the machine, then by all means use one. Just be sure that your corners are exact and that all the other rules for hand sewing are followed (like not stretching edges, making stitches even, etc.).

Stitches

The stitch used to hand sew pieces together is a simple "running stitch," which is the basic sewing stitch. Gather 3 or 4 tiny stitches on your needle, keeping the distance between each stitch even, and pull the needle through. Use whatever size needle and thread is comfortable for you, but keep in mind that a finer needle will make smaller stitches. See Materials and Equipment chapter for further discussion of kinds and sizes of needles and threads.

Take as many stitches on your needle at a time as you can do easily, quickly, and most importantly, *evenly*. The evenness of the stitches is what makes the piecing strong, more so than tiny stitches. Of course, your stitches should be as small as possible. My great-grandmother insisted on doing 20 to an inch. For beginners, try to do 8 stitches as a minimum, 12 if possible.

You can use white or colored thread for almost any patchwork. If your stitches are as small and even as they should be, the color of the thread will not show through. It is not at all necessary to try to match thread color to patch color. The length of stitch, of course, depends to a large degree on the thickness of the fabric you are sewing. Obviously, corduroy or velvet will have fewer stitches per inch than muslin. When I tell you to take even stitches, this means that the stitches on the top side of the seam are the same length as the stitches on the bottom side of the seam. Or that your stitches and the spaces between them are the same. When you come to the end of your row of stitches, secure the row with one or two backstitches. A backstitch *by hand* is done by repeating the last stitch in the row a couple of times. *By machine,* just change the direction of the stitching.

If you are sewing by machine, set your stitch gauge at 10 to 12 for most cottons and similar lightweight fabrics; use longer stitches (or lower number per inch) of 6 to 8 for heavier fabrics like corduroy.

After your pieces are joined together, press the seams closed to one side, not open, which would put more stress on the piecing. Once seams that have been pressed to one side are quilted through, you will have a very strong piece of cloth, even if it is made up of lots of little pieces.

Appliqué Blocks

Many of the principles for assembling patchwork blocks apply to appliqué blocks as well. But there are a few differences and some additional considerations.

Attaching one piece to the top side of another piece requires the use of a stitch other than the running stitch. For appliqué, you can use all the fancy embroidery stitches that you know or would like to learn. If embroidery is not your style, you can use a top running stitch around the edge of the piece being appliquéd; the stitches should be very tiny and regular, since every such stitch will show in this case. Or use a blind stitch, which is the most popular.

First, cut all the pieces that will be appliquéd onto the top of the block. If you are using the whole top of the quilt as a block, follow the same procedure you would follow for a

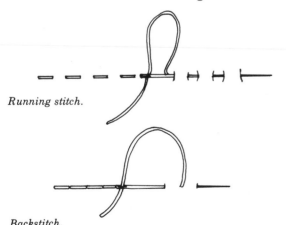

Running stitch.

Backstitch.

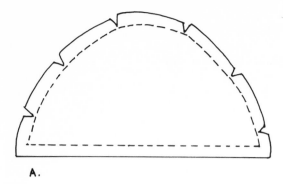

A.

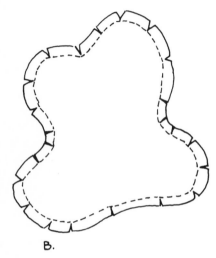

B.

Clip or notch curved edges at regular intervals to reduce stretching or puckering of stitched down edges.

In this Rosebud Wreath quilt block, the stem goes in place first, centered in its foundation square. The large flowers are placed next; then the bud casings, leaving one end open to slip the bud under. The leaves are added last.

smaller block. Pin each piece to be appliquéd to the block in its proper position. If you have difficulty in locating the exact center of the block, fold it in fourths or even smaller pieces and crease it so you can find the center or other key spots for attaching. Never mind the creases; they can be ironed out after the block is finished.

If you have already turned and ironed under the edges for the pieces to be appliquéd, you are ready to sew. If you have not ironed under your seam allowance (which in this case need only be wide enough to stay tucked under after sewing, anywhere from as little as ⅛ to as much as ¼ inch), you must turn under the seam allowance as you stitch the appliqué piece onto its foundation. If you are using circles or arcs, you may need to clip the curves or notch them depending on which way gives you less stress, pucker, and bulk when you have sewn the piece in place.

You needn't turn the edges of pieces that will have other pieces sewn over them. In fact, it makes for a more even-looking finished product if you don't turn these edges under. An example of one piece overlapping another might be a flower sewn over the end of a stem. If you are doing a wreath pattern that has a central circular stem with various leaves and flowers overlapping it, you obviously would not try to turn under only a part of that stem.

Some quilters do prefer to turn under the edges as they sew them down. You will discover which way is most comfortable for you as you work. The order in which you attach the pieces in appliqué follows the same logic as joining patchwork units. The big exception, however, is that it is usually more logical to attach the largest pieces first. Look at a picture of your pattern and study how it should be joined, which pieces should overlap others, etc. Sometimes the flowers should be put down first and the stems and leaves added next. Sometimes, the opposite is the most logical.

For a simple example, look at Moon over the Mountain on p. 13. Attach the moon first because the mountain must overlap the bottom of the moon piece. In the Rosebud Wreath pattern illustrated, the circular stem is the first piece down, then the larger pieces of the circular flowers are sewn over the stem, and then the centers of those flowers are sewn. Then the casings for the buds are stitched on, leaving room at the end to tuck the bud's bottom edge under the top of the bud case and then sew down that last edge. The leaves are added last. All the pieces should be pinned in place before you sew anything, however, to prevent pieces from being improperly placed. This wreath pattern is typical of many appliqué patterns in that design elements repeat themselves at regular intervals and proper spacing between each is most important.

Pinning the piece to be appliquéd is usually all that is needed to hold it in place while sewing. But basting is done more frequently in appliqué than it is in patchwork. If the piece is very large and it slips on the foundation while you sew, you could have a very puckered-looking block with either the top or bottom piece stretched and pulled under the stitches. To prevent this from happening, baste large pieces in place. Keep in mind to baste loosely and with as few stitches as needed. If you are pinning, pin as little as possible, especially if your fabric is a solid color or is backed with Pellon. The pin holes sometimes make permanent holes that show after you remove the pins.

A helpful aid in attaching pieces to a block of appliqué is an embroidery hoop. If you put your block into a large enough hoop, you can attach all the pieces without moving it. And without doing as much pinning and basting, since the hoop keeps the bottom layer of fabric from moving while you sew. Always use thread that matches the top piece being appliquéd.

Blind Stitch

Start on the underneath side of the fabric where your knot won't show. Bring your needle and thread up as close as possible to the turned-under edge of the top piece. Just barely catch the edge of that top piece, going back down under the fabric inside the top fabric edge. This prevents your stitches from showing. Be careful not to make the stitches too tight or the block will look puckered when it is finished.

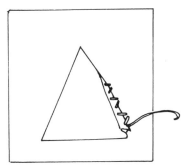

Blind stitch.

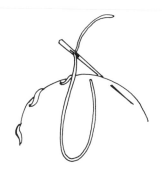

Hemming stitch.

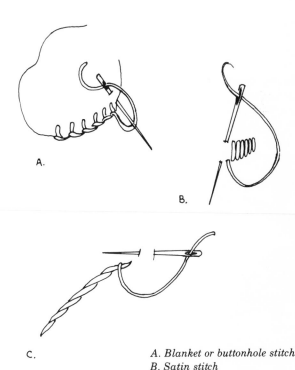

A. *Blanket or buttonhole stitch*
B. *Satin stitch*
C. *Outline stitch*

Hemming Stitch

A hemming stitch can also be used to sew a piece of appliqué. As in the blind stitch, knot the end of the thread and bring the needle up from the underneath side of the fabric, catching the edge of the top piece with the thread. Then go back down over the top of the edge. This stitch is very much like a blind stitch; however, the hemming stitch is done over the top of both layers and not between the two pieces of fabric. This is usually a faster way of sewing, and if you take care to use small, even stitches close to the edge, it is almost as unobtrusive as a blind stitch.

Embroidery Stitches

Any number of decorative stitches can be used to attach your top pieces to the foundation block. An occasional decorative stitch can also be used over the blind or hemming stitch. The most commonly used embroidery stitch for appliqué is the *blanket stitch,* or *buttonhole stitch. Outline stitches* and *satin stitches* are sometimes used. Any of the other embroidery stitches can be used to decorate the plain areas of the block or even some of the appliquéd pieces themselves. Particularly if the design is a "picture style," depicting people or animals, where details in the figure might be embroidered rather than tiny little pieces of appliqué being cut or left out. Even in floral patterns, centers of flowers, leaves, or stems might be done in embroidery stitches. If you like to embroider, let your imagination go to embellish or finish the top of your quilt.

Machine Appliqué

If you want to use the sewing machine to attach your appliquéd pieces, follow the instructions for your particular machine. If it can do various stitches—such as blanket, zigzag, or whatever—you can be decorative while you stitch. This can be a fast and efficient method for completing a block. But remember that machine embroidery will not resemble hand embroidery. The stitches will be very even. Yet, they can be very attractive if done in shades complementary to the piece attached or even if done in contrasting colors or threads.

If you are using your sewing machine for appliquéing, remember to take the same care in pinning and/or basting your pieces in place. In fact, basting is usually more important because the pieces of fabric being appliquéd often slip under the pressure foot or as you turn the fabric. It's better to sew around the edge of the piece with a machine basting stitch before you go around the edge with the embroidery stitch. Machine appliqué can be very attractive, but it is not necessarily faster. Some patterns should definitely be done by hand because they lend themselves to blind stitching, mainly because of its simplicity. The choice is up to you, depending on the pattern you've chosen.

Threads for Embroidery

Earlier I told you to use thread that matched the color of the top piece being appliquéd. However, this does not apply if you are using embroidery stitches that will show intentionally. If you use the same color thread as the piece being stitched, you will create a very lovely and subtle pattern, really adding more texturally than visually. But if you want to add contrast and detail, use either stronger shades of the same color as the piece or lighter shades of a dark color. Or you can use a contrasting color thread to add even more emphasis.

Stuffing

Appliquéd pieces are sometimes stuffed or filled with scraps of batting to create a three-dimensional effect in the pattern on the top of the quilt. This is particularly charming when appliquéing large pieces in the shape of animals or toys for an overall picture on a child's quilt. Curved pieces, rather than those with corners and angles, are better for stuffing since you can enclose the figure more evenly to keep the stuffing from oozing out over time and with many washings.

If you decide to stuff or fill some of your appliquéd pieces, the time to do it, obviously, is when you are sewing the appliquéd pieces to the top of the block. Attach the piece all around, leaving just enough space to push in the filling. The filling should not be stuffed too tightly, or the appliquéd piece will look pulled and stretched.

A block of a Sunbonnet Sue quilt with embroidered details.

10
Setting the Blocks

The *set* of the quilt is the arrangement of the patterned blocks, whether done in patchwork or appliqué. The set creates a pattern of its own and completes the top of the quilt. There are three basic ways for setting together your completed pattern block.

Using All Patterned Blocks

The first way of setting your quilt together is to join patterned block to patterned block. By alternating lights and darks of blocks, new patterns are formed. For example, a typical Log Cabin block is made of contrasting light and dark colors. Depending upon the set chosen, a Log Cabin quilt can be called by several other names, such as Barn Raising, Straight Furrow, Light and Dark, Whirlwind, or Sunlight and Shadow. If the individual blocks are assembled so that half of the block is diagonally in darks and the other half is in lights, you can create any of the other patterns mentioned above when you set the blocks together. Another set that creates patterns of its own is Grandmother's Flower Garden, which is flowers made by rings of hexagons. By clever assortment of lights and darks, other patterns are created by the arrangement of the blocks.

If you have used a variety of colors for the blocks rather than a repeating color scheme within all the blocks, take special care in laying out all the blocks before you join them together. Make sure your design is balanced with an even number of light blocks and dark blocks appearing throughout. If all your blocks are exactly alike, you can sew them together without first laying them all out.

As you sew one block to the next one, be sure to take even seams of ¼ inch. You can join the blocks either by hand or by sewing machine. But if your pattern has square blocks, it is usually much faster to sew the blocks together on the machine. It is a good idea to baste your seams first so that the pressure foot won't catch on any of the pins, and so that all the cross seams will be matched exactly.

Again, if hand sewing, be sure to make very straight, tiny, and even stitches. Don't hurry in seaming the blocks together just because you're anxious to finish the top after all the slow painstaking hours of initial labor. It will seem as though it should be *easy* enough to sew these larger pieces together, but don't hurry so much that you sew unevenly. If you take even a little bit extra seam allowance in joining two blocks and a little less on the next two, your pattern on the top will be all out of line.

As you sew, complete one whole row of blocks at a time. If you make lengthwise rows of blocks, you will have longer but fewer seams to sew on the long edges. When you have finished sewing all the rows, then join the rows together, being very sure to match each seam in one row with the seams in the next one. Carefully pin or baste, whether sewing by hand or machine, so that the seam allowance will be precise and the corners perfectly matched. If you are sewing by hand, you will notice if you slip out of line with matching seams and can correct your error. But if you notice your mistake after completing a machine-stitched row, it will be necessary to take out the machine stitching and do it over.

Using Plain Blocks

The second way of setting your quilt together is to alternate a patterned block with a plain block. The plain block could be white, it could repeat one of the solid colors or prints of the patterned block, or it could be a new color or print that complements the pattern's other colors. Perhaps it should be a neutral color to tone down a very lively arrangement of color and pattern in the patterned block. It might be the same fabric as the border, if you plan one; in fact, many quilts with alternating plain blocks do have borders to unify the completed top. Whatever you decide to use for the alternating plain blocks, the fabric should enhance the other blocks and not overpower them, which is why a neutral color or print is the best idea.

When using this method of joining the blocks, lay out the finished quilt blocks with the plain squares to make sure you have a balanced finished product. If you have an even number of blocks across the top and down the sides, you will have more plain blocks on one side of the quilt than on the other. More impor-

Log Cabin variations. 1. Barn Raising. Quilt courtesy of Barbara Elliman.

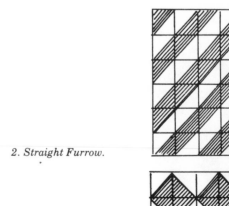

2. Straight Furrow.

3. Light and Dark Variations.

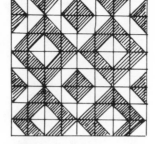

4. Light and Dark Variations.

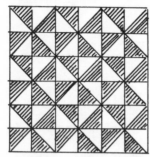

5. Whirlwind.

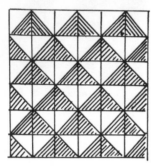

6. Sunlight and Shadow.

Grandmother's Flower Garden variation where patterns are created by the unusual arrangement of colors. Quilt courtesy The Hired Hand.

tantly, the pattern will not look centered when it is on the bed. So it is better to have an uneven number of blocks, at least across the top of the quilt. An even number from top to bottom is not as disturbing, since the bottom row or rows hang down over the end of the bed and since some of the top is usually tucked under the pillows. If you have not taken this into account in your planning, you might want to add another row of blocks down the side to balance things out.

After you have laid out the blocks and are happy with the arrangement, begin sewing them together, following the instructions given for joining patterned block to patterned block. Alternating blocks can be arranged in a checkerboard pattern; or they can be staggered for a very interesting effect. You might group plain and solid blocks by twos or fours. Or you could start with a center block of either the pattern (or the plain) and form a ring around that block with blocks of the alternating plain blocks; in this case, set the blocks from the center out (rather than in rows as explained above).

Lattice Strips

The third way of setting together your quilt blocks is to use lattice strips between the patterned blocks. Lattice strips are anywhere from 2 to 6 inches wide, but they can be any width up to half the width of the block itself. If they are made any wider, they visually become smaller alternating blocks.

Lattice strips run all the way across the quilt and all the way up and down between rows. They can be cut in long strips for one direction; strips running in the crossways direction must be pieced. Or all strips can be cut of equal length and pieced to the blocks as the blocks are joined. Another way to use lattice strips is to cut them to the exact measurements of the patterned blocks and piece them on as if they were borders to the individual patterned block. This leaves little square spaces at the outside corners; the spaces can then be pieced in with squares of a matching fabric or a fabric of another color.

This Starry Crown quilt is set together with lattice strips. Quilt courtesy Paul Rueckwald, Flower in the Crannied Wall.

Pieced block edged with pieced lattice strips. A plain white square fills in each corner where the strips end.

Lattice strips can be in solid colors or dark prints. They can repeat a color or print in the pattern, but they are usually done in a neutral shade to frame the blocks so that each pattern of the patchwork stands out. The print or solid color chosen for the lattice strips is often repeated in the border, if there is one.

Appliqué Quilts

Appliqué quilts sometimes, but not often, have lattice strips joining the blocks together or plain blocks alternating with appliquéd ones. Appliquéd quilts follow the same rules for setting together blocks as patchwork, but most often the pattern that is formed by the appliqué is done against a solid background of white or another neutral color which accents or frames the pattern. In this case, one patterned block is joined to the next, one square at a time, until one row is completed. Then all the rows are attached, and finally the rows are sewn together to complete the top.

When sewing together appliquéd blocks, particularly those with an irregular pattern or a circular motif that repeats itself regularly at the seam edges, you must be very careful in pinning and basting the seam allowances so that the squares will be straight. Or if there is a pattern that continues from one block to the next, take special care to match exactly those edges where the patterns meet.

Appliquéd quilts do not have to be set together at all if they are done with one piece of fabric for the entire background or if the blocks are joined together before being appliquéd. Whichever method seems easier to you is the one you should follow.

Finishing the Set

After you have finished setting all your blocks together, press the seams flat as described for the piecing of the block units. Never press a seam open; it will weaken it. Using a warm setting on your iron, gently press out any wrinkles and creases that have been caused by your sewing. This should be the last time you iron your quilt.

11
Materials and Equipment Other than Fabric

Fabrics for the quilt top and its backing require the most time and care in selection, since they are the most visible parts of the finished quilt. In addition to these fabrics, other supplies are needed to put into the quilt itself, as well as to assemble it.

Batting

The batting, or filler, for the inner layer of the quilt will give the quilt its puffy quality, as well as its warmth. Choose the filler carefully, based on the following: how warm you want the quilt to be; how thick or heavy the batting will make the quilt to sleep under; how easy or difficult the filling will be to quilt through, especially if it is to be hand quilted; how the batting fabric corresponds to the rest of the fabrics in the quilt in terms of cleaning or washing; and finally, what the price is. There are basically four kinds of batting: polyester, cotton, kapok, and down.

Polyester Batting. Polyester batting is the favorite choice of most quilters because it is the lightest in weight and still quite warm. It is machine washable and dryable; in fact, it is better to machine dry it than line dry it because machine drying keeps it fluffy. It will not bunch up over time, and it is easy to sew through.

Polyester can be purchased as polyester fiberfill, which is just a bag of fluffy stuff. It can be bought in five-and-tens or fabric departments or dry goods stores, and it is relatively inexpensive. It is ideal for stuffing pieces of appliqué, pillows, or individual blocks as in biscuit quilting (see Chapter 27). You can vary the thickness of your batting layer as much as you like, but this filling is tricky to work with in a full-sized quilt because it is difficult to make the layer perfectly even.

Polyester batting is also available in sheets and in 45-inch widths by the yard. If you buy the 45-inch batting by the yard, make sure it has been treated or bonded so that it will not bunch or stretch as you work with it. Also make sure that it is flame retardant.

Polyester sheeting is the easiest batting to use for quilting because it requires the least piecing, does not have to be seamed if pieced, won't stretch as you work with it, and seems to stay put after the quilt is finished without extremely close quilting stitches or rows. Mountain Mist polyester batting sheets come in standard quilt thickness (about ¼ inch) in sizes of 81 × 96 and 90 × 108, and in comforter thickness in 72 × 90 sheets. If your quilt is larger or smaller than any of these exact dimensions, you will have to cut and/or piece the batting to fit, but it does not require as much piecing as using 45-inch widths. Mountain Mist batting is sold in many fabric departments and can be ordered from various mail-order supply houses, as well as from the manufacturer (see Sources of Supply).

Polyester batting can also be bought in upholstery thickness, which is several layers of polyester covered with a loose gauzelike covering to prevent breaking apart. It is a little more difficult to find, but try calling wholesalers or upholsterers directly. If they don't sell it, they can at least tell you where to buy it. Upholstery batting is good for making comforters and pillows. It is quite thick and heavy to sew through if you plan a close pattern of quilting. If you simply want a thicker quilt than is possible with one layer of Mountain Mist, use two layers. It is, of course, somewhat slower to quilt through two layers, but it is easier than quilting through upholstery batting.

Cotton Batting. Cotton batting is the second choice of most quilters. It is slightly warmer and makes a thicker and heavier quilt than polyester. It can be bought in sheets or 45-inch widths, and it is often bonded on the outside to prevent its stretching, bunching, or separating as you work with it. However, closer quilting is advisable because cotton swells when wet and will bunch up in the corners over time and with numerous washings. Mountain Mist also makes sheets of cotton batting in 81 × 96 inches and 81 × 108 inches in standard thickness and 72 × 90 inches in comforter thickness. Cotton is less expensive than polyester, and it is better used for smaller quilts and things like toys and pillows than it is for large quilts.

In general, I recommend a single sheet of polyester or cotton batting for most quilts, particularly large ones. For comforters or heavy pillows, use upholstery batting or comforter batting sheets. And for stuffing appliqué or biscuit-quilt squares, use fiberfill.

Kapok and Down Batting. For very specialized quilts or comforters, some people use kapok or down. Kapok is rather coarse and heavy, and it is certainly warmer than polyester or cotton. But it has definite drawbacks because of its texture and weight. Kapok is used for cushions and life jackets. It is difficult to quilt through, but it is warmer than polyester or cotton and much cheaper than down.

Down is a luxurious choice of batting for especially warm quilts and comforters. It makes very thick and puffy quilts that are extremely warm but still lightweight. Some commercial establishments will fill your quilt with down and quilt it, usually by machine. Down is a very expensive filler, but there is none warmer. If you want to use down filling and quilt it yourself, call wholesalers or pillow manufacturers in your area and see how they sell it. In New York, for instance, down is sold by the pound, starting at about fifteen dollars per pound. It will take between 3 and 5 pounds to fill a queen-sized quilt, depending on the quality of the down you use and how puffy you want the quilt to be. If you are interested in down filler, check the Yellow Pages and call suppliers to compare quality and price.

If you want to fill a quilt with down, it is a good idea to make a bag for the down, the size you want the layer of batting to be. Then loosely baste the bag together to keep the layer of down as even as possible while working. It is extremely difficult, if not impossible, to hand quilt a down-filled cover, especially in a traditional method. Even though close stitching or quilting is impractical, you should run parallel lines of stitches both across and up and down the comforter about 8 to 10 inches apart. Or you can make rows of boxes across the comforter or inside one another to keep the down from shifting and bunching up in one area of the comforter. It is easier to stitch up these quilting rows on an industrial machine than on a regular sewing machine or by hand.

Materials and Equipment Other than Fabric   49

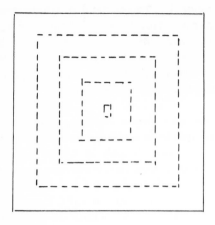

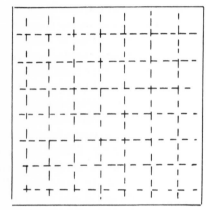

Quilting patterns for down-filled comforters can be rows of stitched boxes inside one another or within interesting straight rows.

Remember that down-filled comforters must always be dry-cleaned. Down is very warm to sleep under and many people find it too warm for comfort in spite of its luxurious feeling.

Quilting Frames

Most people find some sort of frame necessary to hold together the top, batting, and backing layers while the actual quilting is being done—especially if it is being done by hand. A quilt can be hand quilted without any kind of frame, but it requires a great deal of basting to keep the layers from slipping and bunching and to keep the seams from puckering and being uneven. It also requires a great deal of experience with quilting to follow an intricate pattern of stitches. It is also very awkward to hold such a large item in your lap and keep it from getting dirty on the floor as you work.

Frames make quilting much faster and easier, and they make the end result a more evenly stitched quilt. Frames can also be used to baste the quilt prior to quilting. If you are doing any sort of pattern with your quilting

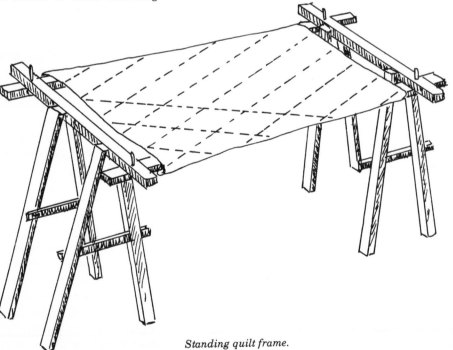

Standing quilt frame.

stitches other than outlining the pattern of the patchwork units or stitching around the appliquéd pieces, a frame becomes even more important. The easiest kind of frame to use is a standing frame large enough to hold the whole quilt while it is being stitched. A standing frame is basically four pieces of wood (2 inches × 2 inches or 1-inch dowels) set together as a frame and raised off the floor to the appropriate height for the quilter to work on while sitting down. In pioneer days, four pieces of wood, joined at the corners to make a rectangle, were rested on the back of chairs, but this is rather unwieldy. The crosspieces can be held together with C-clamps and supported on sawhorses that have been notched to hold the crosspieces securely. Or legs can be fashioned in any way to hold up the frame. The quilt is usually attached to the frame in the following manner. Scrap pieces of cloth, like heavy-duty muslin or canvas, are stapled or nailed to the long sides of the frame or sewn around the sides of the frame. The quilt is then basted to the fabric attached to the long sides of the frame. The quilt is rolled around the side pieces of the frame, leaving a good work area for the quilter, about 18 to 20 inches if one person is going to be quilting and about 35 to 40 inches if two people plan to sit on either side of the frame. The crosspieces can be notched at different distances so that the quilt can be rolled up to allow more or less work area, depending on how much room you have or need to work.

If you have the room to store a large frame when not using it, you can buy readymade frames or order plans for building your own. If you are adventurous you can design and build your own to accommodate special requirements for quilting comfort and space. For example, the long sides must be a few inches longer than the width of the quilt and can be rolled up from top and bottom rather than from side to side. These pieces can be taken apart, if you like, to put the frame away with the quilt still rolled on the side bars and stored between quilting sessions. You should rebaste the ends to the crosspieces each time, however.

The idea is to have your quilt stretched fairly taut in its frame to make the sewing of your

Quilting hoop on a stand.

quilting stitches as easy as possible. The quilt should not be stretched too tight: it should be loose enough for the quilt to move up and down slightly but tight enough to make stitching easy. Even stitches are stronger for quilting just as for sewing the patches together. Even rows are also more attractive when the finished quilt is viewed as a whole. If you are merely following the outlines of your pattern on the top, perhaps you will be more comfortable using a large embroidery hoop. Large round or oval embroidery hoops are available in sizes up to 36 inches across. Stands for these frames can be purchased from needlework specialty stores or ordered from some needlework supply houses. Be sure to buy the kind of hoop that has screw clamps for adjusting the rings rather than the spring type often used for embroidery. Quilting frames should be made to suit your needs, and many interesting things can be done with frames. Some quilters have large frames that are suspended from the ceiling and lowered when in use and raised up for storage. The main reason for using a large frame is to make your work as easy as possible, so construct a frame that will be good for you to work with.

If you use an embroidery hoop, the larger the hoop the less often you have to change its position. Larger hoops are easier to work with, too, in that you can visualize a whole block or area for quilting. One other advantage to hoops is that you can use them to hold your layers together for machine quilting. They are unnecessary and obviously not good if you are doing long, straight rows of stitches either by hand or machine for your patterns.

Needles

Needles are a very important consideration, if you plan on sewing by hand. You need three types of needles. You need one type for straight sewing to seam together the individual units of patchwork and for stitching down appliqué patches to their foundations. (Some people prefer different needles for piecing and for appliquéing depending on what they find comfortable.) The second type is for any decorative embroidery you may want; and the third type is for the actual quilting process itself. Everyone who has done much quilting has his or her own preferences, and what sort of needle to use is a very personal choice. Some people use a quilting needle for all their sewing except for the embroidery stitches.

Straight sewing is usually done with a regular needle, called a sharp, either number 8 or 10. The larger the number, the finer or thinner the needle. The thinner the needle, the easier it is to take very small stitches. A fairly long needle sometimes is preferred, since it allows the sewer to gather more stitches on the needle at one time. Remember, if you are appliquéing, your stitches—and in some cases, your needle marks—will show. One more consideration in needle selection is the size of the eye. You have to rethread needles very often, so choose a needle with an eye big enough to thread comfortably but not so big that your thread keeps slipping out.

Embroidery needles, since they have larger eyes for threading thicker thread, are thicker needles as well. They are regularly packaged in sizes from 3 to 10, with 3 being the largest. Other sizes are available with larger sizes for crewel work.

Quilting needles are short needles, usually very fine, called *betweens*. They are specialty needles that often must be specially ordered from mail-order supply houses specializing in quilting supplies or purchased from specialty departments. As quilting becomes a more popular hobby, the availability of supplies be-

comes greater. Betweens can be bought in sizes from 5 to 10. I find an 8 is a comfortable size to work with. These needles often become curved through use, and some people prefer the curved shape for going down and then up through three layers of material. Curved upholstery needles can be purchased, but they are even more difficult to find than betweens. Betweens are the traditional needles used by quilters, but some people prefer longer needles. For quilts that are tied or tufted, you need a longer and heavier needle, like a tapestry needle, especially if you are tying with yarn. Once again, use whatever is the most comfortable to work with.

Threads

Almost as personal a decision as the choice of needles is the choice of thread. Several kinds of thread are available to the quilter today. I prefer 100-percent cotton, since it does not knot up as easily as polyester-coated threads. However, 100-percent cotton thread of sewing weight is easily found in only white or black, which means it is fine for piecing most units but not good for appliqué where you want to match the color of the piece being appliquéd. For colored thread, Coats & Clarke makes a thread called Dual Duty which is cotton-coated polyester. This thread comes in a wide selection of colors and is supposed to have all the strength advantages of polyester and the smoothness of cotton. It comes in only one weight, which is slightly heavier than a standard sewing weight of 50 but not as heavy as quilting thread. When sewing with any thread, but most especially when sewing with polyester blends, use a fairly short piece of thread about 20 inches long to keep the piece of thread smooth and even while working. Remember about those even-sized stitches.

Another hint is to match the fabric content of your thread to the kind of fabrics you have used. If you have used all cotton fabrics, a polyester thread has a tendency to pucker. The reverse (cotton thread on a polyester fabric is a better but still not a good combination). Mercerized thread is thread that has been treated to make it stronger and to take a dye more evenly.

12
Borders and Bindings

A border is an optional addition to a quilt. If you decide to have one, there are two possible purposes it can serve: (1) to fill out any additional size requirements and/or (2) to frame the pattern on the top of the quilt. Borders are usually added for this latter purpose, since the first reason has obvious limitations.

You can have a plain border, which is obviously the easiest and can be quite effective in setting off an elaborately pieced top. Plain borders can also be very intricately quilted in decorative patterns that either repeat the pieced or appliquéd pattern of the top or that introduce a new pattern to complement it. If this is your first quilt, I suggest using a plain border because it is the simplest.

In planning a plain border, first decide how wide it should be. The best width depends on the size of the patterned blocks. Choose a width that looks good with the top. Then decide how you will finish the corners. They can be mitered, which means joining the cornerpieces in a diagonal line that bisects the angle of the corner. (See instructions for mitering a binding, p. 00.) If you don't miter the corners, they should be squared off carefully where they intersect.

If lattice strips have been used to set together the blocks in the top, use long lattice strips for the border. If you don't want to use a plain border, there are some very simple patterns for piecing borders that are equally attractive with pieced or appliquéd tops. Pieced borders for pieced tops often repeat one of the shapes used in the pattern of the top. They may also repeat one or more of the colors used in the top.

One of the simplest pieced borders is a Sawtooth pattern, which is made up of alternating light and dark triangles (either right angle or isosceles) pieced into long strips. Since most borders are 4 inches or more wide, the sides of the triangles will be long enough to seam on the sewing machine, if you like. In planning a Sawtooth border, first figure the exact length each border strip must be; then figure how many triangles you need per side. Remember that each triangle should be the same size as all the others in the border, with the possible exception of the cornerpiece, and that you must have an exact number, with no half triangles left over, for the pattern to come out correctly. You should also consider how they will meet at the corners. If you have an even number of triangles, your strip will begin and end with different colors. If you have an odd number of triangles per strip, it will begin and end with the same color. See the quilt on p. 000 for an example of a Sawtooth variation border.

If getting your border to come out even at the corners presents a great problem, try using a larger piece of the same shape at the corner, altering the shape, or adding an extra piece on the diagonal. Just be sure to keep the border as consistent-looking as possible.

Another triangle border is called Flying Geese. It is made in strips the same way as the Sawtooth border, but with three triangles of two different sizes making up the pattern. The two small triangles of the lighter color are joined to the sides of the larger dark triangle to form a rectangle. The rectangles are then sewn into strips with the points of the large triangle always pointing in the same direction.

A third pieced triangle border is a Zigzag pattern, which is made by piecing together two rows of alternating light and dark triangles for each border strip, or 8 strips in all. The rows are then sewn together by twos to make the zigzag strip. When joining each two rows for the final strip, line up the point of the light triangle with the midpoint of the base of the dark triangle in the adjoining row. This is easily done if you start the first row with a light triangle and the second row with a dark triangle.

Bindings

Borders for quilts are optional, but every quilt must have a binding to cover the edges of the backing, batting, and top. There are two basic bindings for a quilt.

The backing can be made larger than the top of the quilt, folded over both the batting and the top, then turned under ¼ inch for seam allowance, and then stitched on the top side to finish the quilt. When you use the backing as a border, be sure that the amount turned over and stitched to the top is an even width all along the sides of the quilt. This can be tricky unless you plan a very narrow binding. It is very important to plan this step carefully,

Sawtooth border.

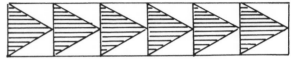
Flying Geese border.

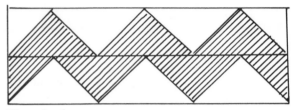
Zigzag border.

since a binding that is even slightly thinner or thicker in spots can spoil an otherwise beautiful top.

The corners of the binding can be mitered. Mitering requires careful matching of the binding strips. The edges of the backing should be turned under a seam allowance depth of ¼ inch and then blind stitched in place around the edge of the top. For the corners, fold back a triangle-shaped piece to mark a straight diagonal line on each end, where the strips meet at the corner, and blind stitch the two ends together.

The binding of the quilt can be a separate strip used to edge the quilt all the way around. Each strip should be cut into four lengths corresponding to the lengths of all four sides of the quilt plus an extra inch or two on all sides for turning and mitering corners. You can purchase bias binding tape in a complementary color to go with the quilt's top, or you can make your own bias binding by cutting strips of cloth 3 inches wide. The strips should be cut either on the lengthwise grain of the fabric or diagonally across the grain of the fabric (or as the term implies, cut them on the bias). The easiest way is to cut or tear along the straight grain of the fabric. But, you can tear these strips only if the grain of the fabric is straight. Since fabric stretches on the bias, binding strips to cover curved or scalloped edges should be cut on the bias. However the strips are cut, they are pieced together to obtain two lengths for the long sides, plus enough for turning and mitering corners, and two widths for the top and bottom plus allowance for corners. It can be a long process to make your own bias binding. Unless you want to try to match a specific fabric used in the top, it is much simpler to use a commercially sold bias binding in a color that will closely match the top of your quilt.

A 3-inch strip of binding will leave only about an inch-wide strip showing on the top because ¼ inch on both sides is turned under for the seam allowance and then the binding is folded so that half is on the top and half is on the back of the quilt. To attach a bias strip of binding to your quilt, first press under ¼ inch for seam allowance and align the right side of the binding with the right side of the top of the quilt. Pin this in place along either one of the sides. Next stitch the seam, either by hand or by machine, being sure to seam the binding to all three layers—top, batting, and backing. Repeat this procedure for all four sides. Then turn the quilt over. Turn under another ¼-inch seam allowance and pin the binding to the back of the quilt, making sure you keep the batting tucked in and the width of the strip even. Also be sure that you have covered the row of stitches already stitched from the top side. You can either miter the corners now or after you have blind stitched the binding to the backing. Personally, I find it easier to do this before attaching the binding to the quilt, because you can unpin one or two pins on the back side's corners to make it easier to work with the binding strips. Now turn under the edges and clip them to a workable width. Next, the seams should be pinned on both top and

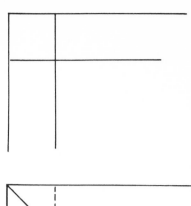

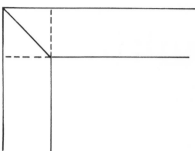

To miter a corner of either a border or a binding, lay the intersecting corner edges over one another as shown. Then fold under on dotted lines and blind stitch on solid diagonal line.

back so that you see a diagonal seam line across the corner. Blind stitch these seams closed. You do not have to miter the corners, but realize that mitered corners are the neatest and *any* corner is tricky to match up. Experiment with bias tape first, if you like, and then find your own preference.

In the long run, good binding is vital to the life of your quilt. Quilts tend to wear out first along their edges, so you may have to replace this binding after a few years. Commercially bought binding tape is probably the most durable of the types mentioned above. If you are making your own binding, it can be as wide as you like. But take this one caution: the wider the binding you use, the more difficult it is to maintain an even width all around.

13
Quilting Methods

Now that you have finished the top, decided on borders, and assembled your backing and batting, you are ready to quilt.

Laying Out the Quilt

First, cut the batting or inner layer to the size of the top. Cut extra strips if the quilt is larger than a standard batting sheet. Choose a work location where the whole quilt can be laid out smoothly for the final step of putting the whole thing together.

It is easier to work on a textured surface. For example, if the quilt is smaller than your bed, you can work on top of it. Or try a carpeted floor. The rough, textured surface keeps the fabrics from slipping around as much as they would on polished surfaces, such as tables or wood floors. You can even pin the backing to the carpet at the corners, but don't overdo the pinning. Remember that you will have two more layers over the top of this piece of fabric, and you won't be able to reach any one of the pins when the time comes to remove them unless they are at the edges of the backing. Also, you do not want to pin or baste the quilt to the bed or the carpet.

First, lay out the backing wrong-side up. Make sure it is perfectly smooth and flat, without wrinkles. Now unroll the batting over the backing, making sure the edges of the batting are flush with the edges of the backing underneath. If you are using a self-binding method for finishing your quilt and need a wider border on the backing side to turn up and over, center the batting inside the backing. If you are intentionally leaving a binding area free to be turned over, then carefully line up the batting the same distance from the edge all the way around. Since batting tends to cling at least slightly to the surface beneath it, the easiest way to place it evenly is to slowly unroll it over the backing. And if you are adding extra strips of batting to fill out an area, it is easier to add as few as possible. Therefore, if you need more batting at the bottom, cut the new piece to fit the area and line it up flush with the larger piece already in place. According to the manufacturer's instructions, there is no need to seam batting, especially the polyesters. However, if you fold the basted quilt or are going to quilt it without a frame, the strips of batting could separate slightly from a lot of handling. This is especially true for polyester batting purchased in 45-inch widths. Be sure to cut each width as long as is possible to reduce the number of pieces. Then when all the needed lengths and pieces are cut, you can whip stitch, loosely baste, or tack at intervals along the touching edges of batting in order to guard against later separation of the batting. Do *not* make a traditional seam in the batting or you will have lumpy areas in your finished quilt. You can tack the strips to one another, then roll up the batting and unroll it over the backing fabric. But when placing it, make sure the batting is perfectly smooth and free of wrinkles.

Now that you have the batting all in place, you must carefully position your quilt top, right-side up, over the two bottom layers of backing and batting. Once you have the top in place and are sure all three layers are carefully lined up, pin the layers together with enough pins to keep them from sliding while you baste. Have pins in the center of the quilt, at the corners, and in the centers of each side.

If you have a large quilting frame, the fastest way to assemble your layers for quilting is to tack the sides of the backing to the edges of the frame. Then add the batting and top. Pin the layers together and baste. If you use a frame, you avoid the risk of basting your quilt to the carpet or bed or, if you have used the floor, the nuisance of everything slipping around as you work.

Basting

I can't overemphasize the importance of basting the *three* layers together before you quilt. Overbasting is a highly unlikely possibility, because no one likes to spend time basting and people usually baste as little as possible. But this is one time when you must baste patiently. Your basting stitches can be long and loose, but numerous rows are needed. The minimum amount you should baste any size quilt, even a pillow, is as follows: there should be intersecting rows through the exact center of the quilt from top to bottom and from side to side. Do these two rows first, starting at the

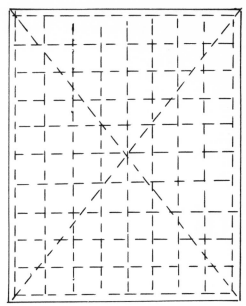

A quilt prior to quilting should be basted with intersecting rows radiating out from the center to the center of the top, bottom, and sides and to each corner. Additional rows both lengthwise and crosswise should be added 10 inches apart.

center and working out to the edges. Then baste diagonal rows across the quilt from corner to corner. These rows should also be done from the center out, carefully smoothing out the batting along with the top and bottom layers to make them flat. After these two rows are basted, add basting rows from top to bottom and side to side about 10 inches apart, again working from the center out. You should end with rows around all four edges of the quilt. These rows of basting will keep your three layers smooth and even as you quilt. If the quilt has wrinkles or lumps at this point, your finished quilt will have them quilted in.

Machine quilting requires the roughest handling of the quilt while working, because you will frequently have to roll, reroll, and move it around to fit under the needle. If you are going to quilt freehand without any sort of frame, the quilt will also demand extra handling. In either case, the quilt should be basted even more than I have suggested previously. Quilts done in hoops need slightly less basting than those done by machine, since part of the quilt is held taut while the rest hangs loose and is free to shift around. Also, as you change the position of the hoop, you may stretch the layers (especially the batting in the middle), allowing the layers to bunch slightly.

Quilts that are to be quilted in frames need the least amount of basting, since the layers are held firmly and evenly in the frame through most of your work. But take special care when first attaching it to the frame and while rolling it up on the sides to change the work area for quilting. These are the points at which stretching can occur. If the quilt will be removed before you're finished, it should be more carefully basted. The 4 intersecting lines through the center are essential for any quilt; plus, you should baste several straight rows up and down and across the center and the outside edges. After you have finished basting, your batting may have been stretched to extend out beyond the edges of the top and backing. If so, trim it carefully with sharp scissors. You don't want any thin or thick spots in the batting.

Even though I have cautioned you to baste many rows, remember that you are not actually quilting with these basting stitches, so make your stitches loose. On large quilts you cannot reach one hand under the three layers and still keep the layers of quilt flat while you work. Therefore, work carefully through the three layers from the top down. Make sure you baste through all three layers, of course.

Marking Your Pattern for the Top

There are several different methods for marking your quilting pattern on the top. To some extent, the marking method is determined by the pattern you plan to use. And to some extent, it is determined by your method of quilting, whether freehand or with an embroidery hoop, standing quilting frame, or sewing machine. And to some extent, it is determined by the implement you use to mark your pattern on the quilt and by your own personal preference.

Some people prefer to mark the top before it has been basted together with the batting and backing, since the batting makes the surface soft and, when marking an intricate pattern,

can distort straight lines ever so slightly. Of course, if you use chalk, it might be erased because of all that handling during the process of basting. For this reason, I suggest marking the pattern after basting together all three layers. Don't use pencil or your marks are likely to be permanent. Even if they will wash out, you shouldn't have to wash your quilt as soon as you've finished it. Use a sharp object. A needle or the point of a compass will scratch a line on the quilt. If you can see this line to stitch along, this is the best way. The marking must be done one section at a time, however. You'll find the marks come off as the quilt is handled.

If you can't see the line well enough to quilt by, go over it with chalk. The chalk will usually stay in the indentation of the scratched line and will brush off easily when you have finished. A good way to mark a straight line with chalk is to secure one end of a string with chalk and then secure the other end to the opposite side and snap the string, leaving a chalk line across the quilt.

Some patterns do not have to be drawn on at all. If you are tracing the outlines of your patterned blocks, you already have lines to quilt around. If you have only certain areas to be quilted in a pattern, other than those formed by the pattern of the top, you can mark these areas of the quilt as you come to them. Also, overall arrangements of straight, parallel lines are best marked lightly before attaching to a frame, but they can be more clearly marked as you quilt. The trick here is to keep each row straight and parallel with the preceding row. You can use the chalked-string method already described, or you can use a yardstick with chalk or a tracing wheel. In fact, tracing wheels are excellent for marking outlines for even the most complicated pattern.

Putting the Quilt in a Frame

Now that you have finished basting, you are ready to attach the quilt to its frame. If you have not already done so, attach sturdy strips of cloth. These can be bias tape, canvas, heavy denim, muslin, or whatever scraps you may have. Secure these strips to the wooden frame on both of the long sides; they can be nailed or stapled into the wood, or they can be folded around all sides of the bar of the frame and then sewn together. Next baste your quilt to these strips, again using long, loose, basting stitches. Then roll your quilt around the bars until it is taut and a comfortable work area has been created to begin quilting in. There is no need to baste the other two edges to the cross bars, especially if you are rolling the quilt at the sides and there is a relatively short distance between the side bars. If your work area is large enough for the quilt to sag significantly or if you have used especially heavy batting, you can baste the crosswise sides of the quilt to their adjacent bars if it helps to keep the working surface taut. Of course, every time you roll the quilt, you will have to rebaste these ends.

When quilting a quilt that is stretched on a standing frame, choose the direction you work in with your stitches according to whatever is most suitable for your pattern. You can work from one side to the other or from top to bottom, depending on how you have attached the quilt to the frame. If the long sides of the quilt are attached to the long bars, you will probably be working from top to bottom for one row of the pattern and then rolling your quilt and quilting another row of the pattern from top to bottom. Some quilters prefer to work from the center out in all cases. If your pattern is based on a central design, radiating out from the center of the quilt, then you must quilt from the center out to ensure that your quilting pattern is centered. If, however, your pattern of quilting stitches is a repetition of the block pattern, or one of the parallel line patterns, then it does not matter at all which direction you quilt in or where you start or finish.

Using a Hoop for Quilting

If you use a quilting hoop, it is usually helpful to mark a large pattern or rows of lines before you start. You should always quilt from the center out if you use a hoop or if you're not using any kind of frame at all. If you move from the center out, you will keep the smoothing of the three layers ahead of you and will prevent bunching or wrinkling of the batting or backing.

Quilting on the Machine

You should roll the sides of the quilt into tight, flat rolls to facilitate getting the extra body of the quilt between the needle and the machine itself. Take care not to stretch the area being rolled by trying to roll too tightly. You should, of course, have your pattern clearly marked on the top before you begin sewing. If you are very experienced with a sewing machine and have the kind of machine that can be maneuvered easily, then by all means use your machine for quilting. Just remember that the main difficulty in machine quilting is constantly turning and moving large amounts of three-layered material around. Very close hand basting is vital when machine quilting. If you are outlining the pattern of the individual pieces of the patterned blocks, it may require some very fancy machine stitching, and hand quilting is probably much neater as well as easier. An embroidery hoop around the part of the quilt to be worked on can be eased under the pressure foot if attached to the quilt upside down. This helps hold the layers taut while machine stitching, but it is just one more thing to be moved and adjusted as you sew.

If you machine quilt, it is best to work from the center out for the same reasons described for hoop quilting.

The Quilting Stitch

In effect, a quilting stitch is a series of running stitches, the same type used to join units of patchwork together. However, you usually begin by doing only one stitch at a time. Use as fine a needle as you find comfortable to work with and a length of thread about 20 inches long, knotted at one end. Starting on the underside of the quilt, pull the knot of the thread through the layer of backing into the batting (where it should remain so that the knot won't show). Then come up through the layer of the batting and top with the needle and thread. Put the needle down very close to the point where the thread comes up through the layers and penetrate all three layers of top, batting, and backing and come back up

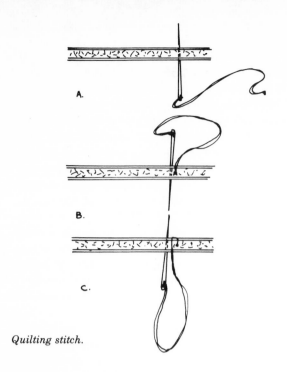

Quilting stitch.

through the three layers again. One hand is usually holding the needle on the top side of the quilt. The other hand is usually held underneath the layers to make sure the needle comes all the way through the three layers. That hand then guides the needle back up a short distance away from where it emerged from the material. You will obviously need a thimble for the hand on the underside. Quilting stitches, like running stitches for piecing, should be as small as possible and, most importantly, as even as possible. You can take as many stitches at a time as you find comfortable to do, but each time you should complete at least one full stitch from top to bottom and up to top again. Take as many stitches per inch as possible. Remember, the finer the needle, the easier it is to make small stitches. It is said that experienced quilters can do 12 or 14 stitches per inch. For your first quilt, 8 stitches per inch is quite good. Try for at least 6. When you reach the end of your length of thread, don't try to stretch it out and pull the thread too tightly. Be sure to end your length of thread with a few tiny backstitches to secure the end. *And don't leave your needle in the fabric when you're not quilting. It might mark it.*

Keep the lengths of thread being worked with short, so they don't tangle or knot. This means threading your needle often, but the

evenness of your stitches will be quite noticeable in the end product. Remember, quilting stitches are the ones that show. Another help in keeping that thread smooth and those stitches even is a coat of beeswax on your thread. The wax also makes the thread stronger and less likely to tangle or break as you work. When making quilting stitches, do not pull your thread too tightly or it might break. At the very least, it puts too much stress on the stitch and the fabric in-between. Keep the stitches firm enough to make a slight indentation in the top where the row is complete. Keep even tension on your thread at all times.

As you work a row of quilting stitches, the batting has a tendency to bunch a bit. Keep the pressure of your hands gentle to reduce that bunching. At the same time work the bunching slightly ahead of your needle if it is more than you can smooth out evenly as you work. The arrangement of one hand on top and one underneath is helpful in smoothing gently as you work. If there are several of you sitting in a row to quilt one long stretch, be especially careful not to end one section with a lump of extra batting or you will have that lump as a permanent part of your finished quilt. How close together your rows of quilting stitches should be is largely a matter of taste; but you should also take into consideration your choice of batting, the pattern you have chosen for the quilting, the pattern of your top, the overall size of the piece being quilted, and your enthusiasm for quilting.

In the early days of quilting, when cotton batting was the traditional filler, good quilters felt that no more than 1 inch should be left unquilted, for appearance as well as to prevent the batting from shifting around or swelling and breaking the stitches when the quilt was washed. Some rows were less than ½ inch apart. Today, with polyester batting in sheets used for most quilt fillings, one does not really have to quilt closer than 4 inches between rows. If you have a small, intricately worked patchwork pattern that you are outlining, the pattern will probably determine the distance between stitches. But if you have used cotton batting in sheets, you should quilt at least every 2 inches. If you are quilting a pillow or a small quilt for an infant, let the visual effect determine how close you quilt the piece. In the small area of a pillow, the batting doesn't have very much room to move around anyway. In a small crib quilt, a closer design will probably be in keeping with the design of the top.

If you are quilting on your sewing machine, set the stitch gauge to 6 to 8 per inch. This depends on the thickness of your batting and the weight of the top and bottom layers. The thicker the layers, the fewer stitches you should have to the inch. Loosen your tension from that for ordinary sewing so that your stitches will be even. Do some practice rows on an equivalent thickness to make sure the tension is set correctly or your quilting will start to pull out almost as soon as you've finished it. Keep the pressure foot up to reduce the pulling or stretching of the batting, but be very careful to keep the fabric moving under the needle evenly. The part of the quilt outside the needle is heavy and needs to be supported or else its weight could distort your pattern of stitches. Prop the extra unworked-on areas of the quilt on a table set close by your machine.

Quilting Patterns

When working quilting rows on a machine, long, straight rows of stitches worked either lengthwise and crosswise or diagonally from corner to corner are the easiest patterns to do. You might try parallel rows of stitches going in one direction only, which will form stripes in the direction you quilted them. This can be an interesting pattern all by itself. If you follow this plan, your rows should be about 2 or 3 inches apart unless you have used very heavy batting and it is impossible to quilt that close together. If you stitch rows first in one direction and then in a perpendicular direction, you will form either little squares or diamonds over the top of the quilt. In this case you need to have your rows only 4 or 5 inches apart for most polyester or cotton batting of average thickness.

Patterns for Hand Quilting

The most popular pattern to follow for hand quilting is repetition of the pattern within the blocks of the top. This is true for both patch-work and appliqué patterns. Simply outline the pattern pieces in the block. If your pattern is appliqué, this is usually done around the outside of each piece very close to its edge so that the piece stands out slightly from the background fabric. If your pattern is patch-work, your pattern will determine where the best quilting lines should go. If your pieces are small and self-contained (such as hexagons, Log Cabin rectangles, or diamonds), the most common quilting pattern is to stitch inside each piece about ¼ inch from the seam. *Never quilt through the seams.* This will weaken them. But if you stitch close to the seam, either on the outside or inside of the pattern unit, it adds strength to the quilt.

If a set of alternate plain and patterned blocks has been used, the plain blocks are often quilted in the pattern of the patchwork or appliqué square, such as Moon over the Mountain. The quilting stitches in the plain block repeat the pattern of the patched block but only in relief.

If you have an overall pattern to your quilt, such as in a Lone Star quilt, you will have large areas without pattern that can be filled with whatever pattern of quilting stitches you prefer. You can impose a geometric pattern of parallel lines, continue the points of the star radiating out toward the corners, or use your fanciest stitch of quilt swirls and stars.

Some quilters adhere to the theory that if your top pattern has straight lines and angles, your quilting pattern should use curved lines. And that if you have a pattern of curves and floral wreaths in your quilt's top pattern, you

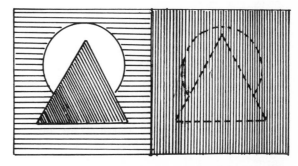

Some quilting patterns both accent and outline the pattern of the top. Sometimes plain alternating blocks are quilted in the pattern of the patterned block to repeat the pattern in relief.

should use straight lines. However, there are just as many quilters who firmly believe that if you use straight lines in the pattern for the top, you should use a quilt pattern made of straight lines.

As you can imagine, there are about as many quilting patterns as there are quilters. My advice is to pick a simple pattern for your first quilt. It will take a while to get used to making even quilting stitches. Some of the most deceptively simple straight line patterns can be quite difficult if they extend over the whole top of the quilt.

If you look in any book of patterns or at any number of finished quilts—especially antique quilts—you will find a wealth of ideas for patterns to duplicate or adapt for your own quilt. Many mail-order supply houses stock unusual and antique patterns complete with stencils or printed patterns for tracing. Or if you like, design your own.

Tufting

Tufting or tying has become an increasingly popular method of joining the three layers of your quilt. This is a simpler and much faster method than traditional quilting. Tying or tufting does not require the use of frames, but hoops are helpful.

What is tying or tufting? It is the process by which yarn or heavy thread, of buttonhole or carpet weight, is stitched at regular intervals through all three layers of the quilt to form little tufts. They keep the batting, top, and bottom together while the ends of the threads are left long to show. The ties or tufts can show on either the top or bottom of the quilt, whichever you prefer.

The process is quite simple. Use a heavy needle, one with an eye big enough for the tufting thread to fit through. Make sure the three layers of quilt are taut and even. Using an embroidery hoop helps.

Use heavy-duty thread and start on the side of the quilt you plan to finish on, or in other words, start on the side you want the ends to show on. Do not knot your thread. Take the needle and a double thickness of thread down through all three layers of quilt, making sure

Tied stitch.

to leave enough thread on the top side to use for tying—about 3 or 4 inches. Take a stitch about ¼ inch long on the underneath side and then bring the needle and thread back up to the top. Make sure not to go inside a seam with your tufting. You can then take another stitch through all three layers over this one or cross it. But come back up to the top again and tie off the thread, making a double knot. Then clip the ends to the desired length.

If you have used heavy-duty button or carpet thread, and it is not very attractive when left showing, tie a piece of colorful yarn in the stitch. You can make the entire stitch with yarn if you like. Just be sure to use a yarn that is fairly strong. A contrasting color is often chosen for the yarn to provide an accent for the quilt top. The tufts should be spaced equidistantly on the quilt. In the old days, they were 1 inch apart. Today, spacing them 2 or 3 inches apart will do if you are using modern sheet-style polyester. Make sure the spacing is *even* and that the tufts won't interfere with the pattern of the quilt top.

Biscuit Quilting

One more way to simplify the quilting process is to quilt each square as you go. The biscuit quilt in Chapter 25 is a good example of this method.

Other more traditional patchwork patterns can be done one block at a time and quilted before setting together. If you choose this method, you can join the blocks by overcasting the edges of the blocks together. Or you can join them with thin lattice strips which can be machine stitched on one side and blind stitched on the other to hide the stitching. If you don't mind the stitches showing, you can carefully machine top stitch the strips in place.

Part II
Patterns

14
Squares with Triple Border

There is no quilt easier to make than this one. The dimensions of the finished quilt illustrated are 88 × 98. The basic pattern unit is a 5-inch square. There are 12 squares across the quilt and 14 lengthwise, which makes for a total of 168 squares. The dimensions of the patterned area are 60 × 70. Three 4-inch borders in bright solid colors of green, blue, and orange are then added to increase the dimensions to 84 × 94. When the 2-inch dark-blue border/binding is added, it fills out the quilt's area to 88 × 98.

Each square should be cut 5½ inches × 5½ inches to allow ¼ inch for seam allowance on each side. The quilt illustrated is made from a random pattern of scrap fabrics. A total of 3¼ yards of 45-inch fabric or 4½ yards of 36-inch fabric is needed for all the squares. For the best effect, use several different colors for the squares. A 6-inch-wide strip of 45-inch fabric will yield eight 5½-inch squares. The same width strip in 36-inch material will yield six 5½-inch squares. One example of planning repeating colors would be to use a combination of 7 different prints, for which you would need ½ yard of 45-inch fabric for each print. This would yield 24 squares for each of the 7 fabrics. If you used 36-inch material, you would need 10 different fabrics of ½ yard to cut all the squares for this quilt. One-half yard of 36-inch fabric yields 18 squares.

Borders

Each border has a finished width of 4 inches. You need to cut 5-inch strips (½-inch seam allowance) for the borders as follows:

Border 1. 2 strips 5 × 69 inches and 2 strips 5 × 79 inches.
Border 2. 2 strips 5 × 77 inches and 2 strips 5 × 87 inches.
Border 3. 2 strips 5 × 85 inches and 2 strips 5 × 95 inches.

Two binding strips are cut 5 × 89 and 5 × 99. This combination border and binding has ½-inch seam allowance on each side; 2 inches show on the front and 2 inches show on the back.

This is a very simple pattern to adapt to any size you wish. By decreasing each square to 4 inches you can produce a quilt 76 × 84. Or you can increase

Squares with Triple Borders quilt is made from 5-inch squares edged with 3 borders for a finished size of 88" × 98". Quilt courtesy Paul Rueckwald. Flower in the Crannied Wall.

the number of rows of squares across or up and down. The quilt is assembled by joining long rows of squares and then sewing together the rows themselves. This type of quilt is known as a strip quilt. It is very simple to do on the sewing machine, because the squares are large enough and there are no corners to turn since you are sewing only one seam at a time. You must take the time to sew carefully, nonetheless, because it is important to make each square the same size as the next one for an even pattern.

15
Baby Blocks

This pattern is really quite simple to make, although it looks most elaborate when finished. Its finished size is 74 × 86; the pieced area is 56 × 68 with a 9-inch border all around. There are 287 pieces in the top. The basic unit of this quilt is a diamond of 4 inches per side. The quilt illustrated has been made with scrap fabrics with no specific repetition of color or print.

However, there are three classifications in terms of color intensity, which must be followed to make this pattern work out. Three diamonds are sewn together to form a cube and three levels of colors are needed to give the cube its dimensional effect. A light color or print (A), a medium shade (B), and a very dark color or print (C). If you wish to make this quilt with the same three colors in each cube, just follow the three color levels described for the scrap quilt illustrated. The darkest shade is the top, the medium shade is the left side, and the lightest shade is the right side throughout the entire quilt.

When selecting the three colors, use the same arrangement of diamonds to form each cube. In other words, if you use a dark diamond for the top of the cube and the medium diamond for the left side, and the light one for the right, always repeat that order to achieve the dimensional cube effect of the total pattern.

The Cubes

To make this quilt you need 83 cubes and 10 half cubes. You need 259 diamonds—88 light (A), 88 medium (B), and 83 dark (C). To make 1 cube, sew together 2 diamonds—1 light (A) and 1 medium (B) shade. When finished, the light diamond should be on the right side of the cube as you look at it.

To join diamonds, place the right sides together and pin at the corners. The edges will not match exactly but should extend slightly at the tips. If you match the points exactly at the edges and then seam, the 2 diamonds will look matched when you open them, but you will lose some length in each side. If you wish to leave templates or paper patterns in place after cutting diamonds, turn and baste seam allowance, then sew together diamonds matching points exactly. To finish the cube, attach a dark diamond (C) to the top on 2 of its sides as shown. The point on the bottom sides of C must match exactly at the seam line joining A and B. You need to make 83 cubes in this fashion.

You then need 10 half cubes to fill in the odd rows of the set. These half cubes are made as follows. Each of the 10 half cubes consists of 1 full-sized diamond (5 light and 5 medium) and 1 triangle of the dark fabric for the top. This triangle (D) is half of a diamond, cut across the short center line of the diamond, with an added ¼ inch for seam allowance on the cut end. You need 10 of these triangles, cut from the dark fabric.

To form these half cubes, first join 5 of the dark triangles to the 5 light diamonds (A), keeping in mind that these half cubes will be used along the left side of the quilt. The dark triangle should be the top of the cube and should have its flat base on the left side and its point meeting the point of the A triangle on the right side after it is finished. For the other 5 half cubes, you reverse this direction to sew the remaining 5 dark (D) triangles to the medium-shade diamonds. The flat side of the finished triangle should be on the right with the point of the dark triangle meeting the point of the medium diamond on the left.

To finish out the top and bottom rows of the quilt, you need 2 more pattern pieces, both triangles, E and F. Triangle E is half a diamond (with the diamond being cut in half lengthwise) with a seam allowance added to the cut side. You need 7 E triangles in the dark print and 7 triangles in either medium or light.

These triangles are added to fill in the spaces on the top and bottom of the quilt.

The last pieces to be added are those for the corners. These are the F triangles, which are made from half of either the D or E triangles, plus a seam allowance on the cut edge. You should have 2 dark and 2 light or medium.

Fabric Amounts

For each of the 3 shades of fabric, you need 1¾ yards each of 45-inch or 2½ yards each of 36-inch fabric to cut all the diamonds and triangles.

The Set

The cubes are joined in rows, working from left to right with the right side of one cube joined to the left side of the next cube across one whole row. If you are left-handed and wish to work from right to left in joining cubes, join

Baby Blocks quilt made from diamonds. Quilt courtesy the firm of Thos. K. Woodard: American Antiques & Quilts.

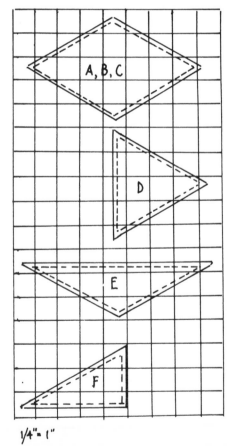

¼" = 1"

When sewing together diamonds along the edges, the points should not line up exactly, but rather extend slightly on each end so that no distortion of size or shape occurs after the two pieces are stitched and then opened up.

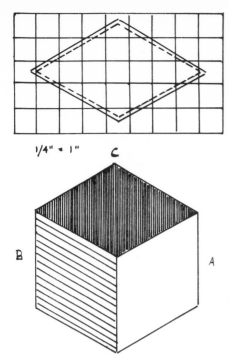

1/4" = 1"

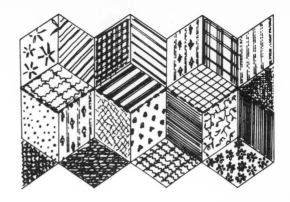

To complete 1 row, join cubes with light right sides to medium left sides. The odd rows are done in this way. Even rows begin with cubes of dark tops and light sides. When row 1 is joined to row 2, the bottom points of the cubes should fit exactly into the V created by the seamed sides of the row below.

To make 1 complete cube of Baby Blocks, sew together one light color diamond and one medium color diamond so that when finished and looking at the right sides, A is on the right and B is on the left. The top is added to the cube by sewing in place the C (dark) diamond. Be sure to match the side point of the C diamond exactly with the points of the A and B diamonds.

the left side of one cube to the right side of the next cube.

This first row is made up of 8 whole cubes. The sides of the cubes are joined just as the sides of the diamonds that form the cubes were done.

When assembling rows, remember to keep the cubes right-side up. For the quilt illustrated, this means keeping the dark side on top.

First, assemble row 1 by joining a light right side of the first cube to the medium left side of the next cube until 8 whole cubes have been joined. To assemble the second row, join 7 whole cubes in this fashion and then add a half cube (made with a light diamond) to the left end and a half cube (made with a medium diamond) to the right end. Complete all 11 rows in this way.

To join row 1 and row 2, align all the center seams of the cube sides. You will be joining the bottom of a medium left side to the right side of a dark triangle top, then a light right side to the left side of the dark top of the first complete cube in row 2. Join all the rows together. Then fill in the corner triangles and the filler E triangles on the top, matching point to point.

Then fill in the E triangles on the bottom row and the top is completed.

You may prefer to piece the corners and filler triangles to the top and bottom rows after you have completed the individual rows and before you join the rows.

The Border

This quilt has a solid color border 9 inches wide all around, which makes a very nice frame for the quilt. You need 4 finished borders; 2 that are 68 inches and 2 that are 74 inches long. The corners of this quilt are not mitered to square it. If you wish to miter the borders, make the top and bottom borders 74 inches finished (75 with seam allowance) and the side borders 86 inches finished (87 with seam allowance at each end).

The binding and the backing of this quilt match the border fabric.

Quilting

The quilting pattern is quite simple. Each diamond is first quilted ¼ inch inside the seam line of each piece. Then it is stitched with 2 intersecting lines inside each diamond to form 4 diamonds to accent the cube pattern of the patchwork. The border is quilted with parallel diagonal lines 2 inches apart and intersected by diagonal lines to form a diamond pattern again repeating the design of the top. As you can see from the illustration, each border strip is quilted as a single strip.

16
Roman Stripe

The finished size of this quilt is 94 × 118. Each block is 8 inches square and is made up of 4 rectangles 2 inches by 8 inches. There are 11 blocks across and 14 lengthwise. That means 154 blocks or 616 pieces in the quilt. There is a 3-inch plain border on all 4 sides. This quilt is big enough for a king-sized coverlet or a queen or double spread. The quilt illustrated is made of a random arrangement of scrap pieces of fabric.

The Block

To assemble each block, first cut strips 2½ × 8½ inches. Sew together 4 strips along their long edges, using ¼ inch for seam allowance. After you have assembled all 154 blocks, sew them together so that each block's stripes are perpendicular to the stripes in the next block. Make long rows of blocks, beginning the first row of 11 blocks with strips going crosswise joined to ones going up and down. Make 7 of these rows. Then make 7 rows starting with blocks where strips run up and down. Then seam together the long rows, alternating the directions of the strips and carefully matching seams.

This is a very good pattern for machine sewing, since the strips are long enough and you need sew in only one direction at a time, which requires no turning of corners. This pattern is also very easily adapted to any size, since it is simple to add or subtract rows without changing the overall effect of the pattern.

Quilting

The illustrated quilt is tied with red yarn ties at 4-inch intervals. If you prefer a hand-quilted pattern, the most traditional is to outline each strip ¼ inch inside the seams of each strip.

A striking quilt design is made by repeating the same colors in every block. To make such a pattern, you need 2½ yards of each of 4 colors in 45-inch fabric or two ¾ yards of 36-inch fabric. Then follow the same order of color in each block.

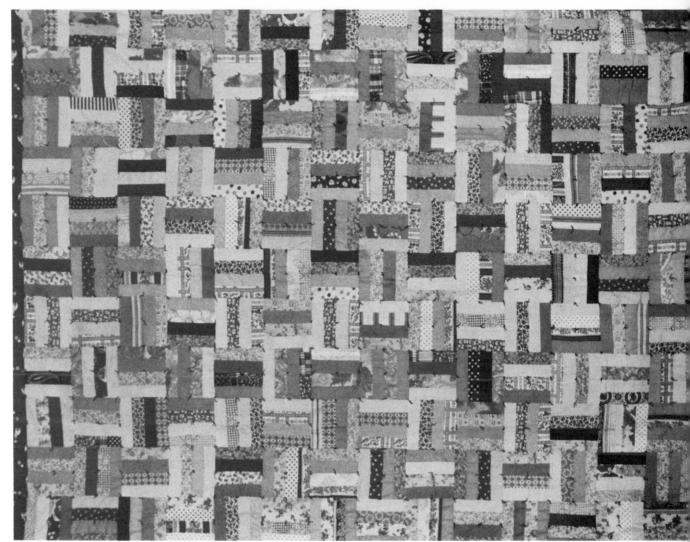

Roman Stripe quilt, made of random scrap fabrics. Each
8-inch square block is made of four 2 x 8-inch rectangles.
Quilt courtesy Caroline R. MacNichol.

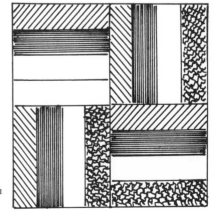

*The changing direction of the stripes from block to block in
the set of a Roman Stripe forms its overall top pattern.*

17
Dresden Plate I

This very old pattern is really a combination of patchwork and appliqué. The plates are pieced together and then appliquéd onto a foundation block. There are two quilts of this pattern illustrated. One is a large quilt with a finished size of 64 × 80, which can be used as a blanket on a twin bed. There are 20 plates making up the quilt top. Each plate consists of 20 petal-shaped pieces, pieced around a center circle 4½ inches (finished size) in diameter. Each petal is 4½ inches long at the longest point (each wide end is curved) and varies from ⅞ inch at the base to 2 inches at the wide end. All petal dimensions are finished size. (For cutting, add ¼-inch seam allowance on all edges.)

There are 20 blocks for a total of 420 pieces, not including background squares, in the quilt. Each petal is appliquéd to a 16-inch white base.

To piece each block, pin all the petals to one another allowing ¼ inch for seam allowance and then sew these strips together to form the plate. The circle is then stitched into the center. Each plate is then appliquéd to its foundation. If you prefer to use a solid piece of background fabric, then be sure to pin each plate in place before appliquéing to make sure the plates are evenly spaced across the top.

A larger variation of this quilt, 80 × 100, can be made simply by enlarging the foundation squares from 16 to 20 inches. The plate size can stay the same. Or you can increase the number of blocks in the quilt. Or you can enlarge the plates, as well as the blocks they are appliquéd to.

Quilting

A traditional method of quilting is to quilt inside the petals and then stitch intersecting straight lines across the center circles, as in the quilt illustrated. If you are a little more adventurous, a particularly lovely quilting design is made by stitching concentric circles inside the center circle and concentric scalloped circles around the plate to the edges of the foundation block. For the quilt illustrated, each of the plates was outlined around the appliquéd line and then a floral design was quilted in the white spaces between blocks. Finally, a floral leaf pattern was quilted in the smaller white areas between the plates.

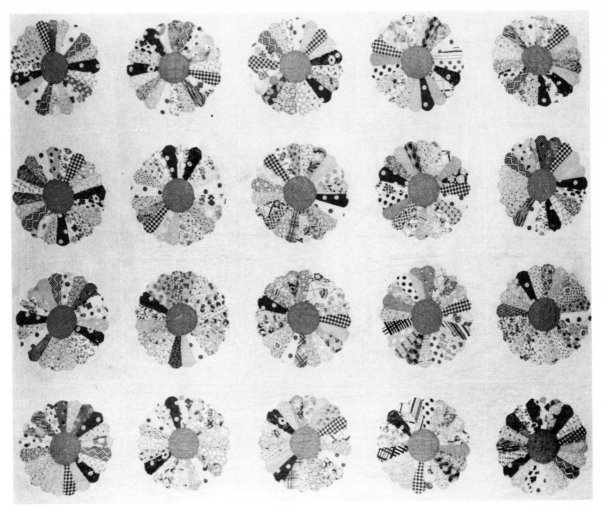

This Dresden Plate quilt is a very popular pattern which combines piecework with appliqué. Quilt courtesy Lisa Johnson Fleck.

Fabric Amounts

Scraps of many fabrics are used for this pattern. Sometimes a fabric is repeated only once in each plate. If this is the plan, you will need 21 different scraps—20 for 1 petal per plate and 1, traditionally a solid color, for the center circles. A 10-inch strip of either 36- or 45-inch fabric is enough for each of the 20 petal pieces, and a 15-inch strip of either 36- or 45-inch is enough for the 20 center circles. If you want to repeat a petal, you need ½ yard of either 36- or 45-inch fabric for each of the 40 petal pieces. For the foundation blocks, you need 4¾ yards of either 36- or 45-inch white fabric.

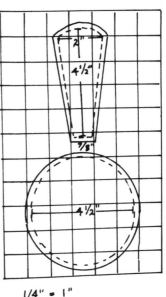

1/4" = 1"

18
Dresden Plate II

The baby quilt illustrated is made up of six 11-inch squares of 10-inch plates, which are composed of fifteen 4-inch-long petals around a 2-inch circle. There are 96 pieces in the pattern and 5 lattice strips, for a total of 101 pieces. The width of the petals varies from ⅔ inch at the base to 2 inches at the widest point. All pattern-piece dimensions are finished size. For cutting, allow ¼ inch around each pattern piece for seam allowances.

The finished appliquéd blocks are joined by lattice strips of bright-red calico, and the whole quilt is framed by a border of the same red calico. The unusual thing about this quilt is that the crosswise lattice strips and border strips are 4 inches (finished size, 4½ inches for cutting size with ¼-inch seam allowances), while the middle long strip and the long borders are 7 inches finished width (7½ inches for cutting widths). The overall dimensions of this quilt are 43 × 49.

Fabric Amounts

The 2-inch circles of each plate are of the same calico as the lattice strips and borders of this quilt. For unpieced borders, lattice strips, and circles, you need 2¾ yards of 36-inch or 2 yards of 45-inch fabric. If you use a different fabric for each of the 15 petals and repeat the pattern in each of the 6 plates, you need 6 petals of each fabric. Six petals can be cut from ⅛ yard of either 36- or 45-inch fabric. For background squares, cut 11½-inch squares (allow ¼-inch seam allowance); you need ¾ yard of 36- or 45-inch fabric.

The fabrics used in this quilt are very bright and lively. The design and pattern can be adapted to a larger size by adding more rows of plates and lattice strips in both directions. The 11-inch block is large enough to be used in a larger quilt.

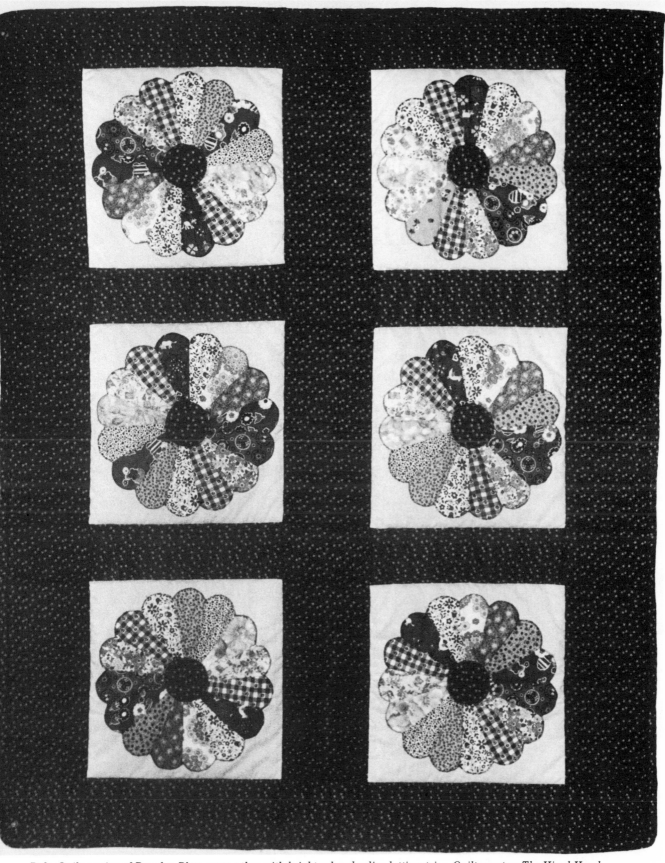

Baby Quilt version of Dresden Plate set together with bright colored calico lattice strips. Quilt courtesy The Hired Hand.

19
Grandmother's Flower Garden I

There are two variations of the pattern illustrated here. The first one, Grandmother's Flower Garden I, is the simpler one. It is made of a total of 413 pieces. The basic pattern unit is a 2-inch hexagon. The finished quilt is 32 × 48 inches.

The quilt illustrated has used very bright colors to make each flower, alternating solid colors and prints in each ring. Each ring is made up of only one fabric for the entire ring. There are 19 hexagons in each of the 11 complete flowers: 1 of Color A, 6 of Color B, and 12 of Color C.

This is an ideal pattern for using small amounts of fabric, since the largest number of pieces to be cut from any one fabric is 12. One row 3 inches wide of 36-inch fabric is all that is required to cut twelve 2-inch hexagons. A 12-inch square of fabric will cut 16 hexagons. You may want to repeat a fabric in one of the partial flowers that fill in the sides or the top and bottom.

You need a total of 209 hexagons to complete the 11 full flowers, 76 hexagons to complete the partial flowers that are used to fill in the rows, and 128 white hexagons to join all the flowers.

The partial flowers are made as follows. The center of the top and bottom rows are half flowers, made up of a center hexagon, 4 of the next ring, and 7 of the outer ring. Use whole hexagons to make the partial flowers and then trim as necessary when adding the binding.

You also need 6 partial flowers to fill in the sides of the quilt. These partial flowers are made up of 1 center hexagon and 5 around the center. The corners of the quilt are filled in with 1 center hexagon and 3 around it.

The Set

Lay out your hexagon flowers and choose the placement of the flowers that you like best. Then attach a ring of 18 white hexagons around the 4 flowers you have chosen for the corners. Then starting with the left long row of 4 flowers, attach the second flower at the top to the white border hexagons at the bottom of the first or upper left-hand flower. Then add 14 white hexagons to encircle this flower and attach the next flower at its top to the center white hexagons at the bottom of the second. This third flower can now be attached on its bottom

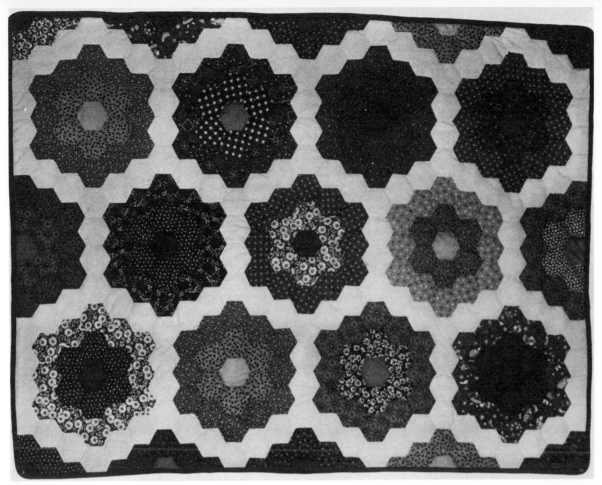

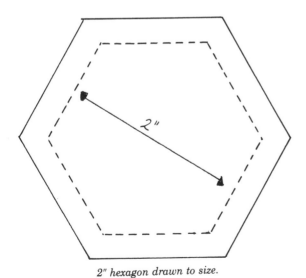

This Grandmother's Flower Garden baby quilt is made in very bright colors. Quilt courtesy The Hired Hand.

2" hexagon drawn to size.

side to the last hexagon in the row, which has already been encircled with white hexagons. Next, fill in the empty spaces around this third flower with 10 white hexagons. Follow this same procedure for the right-hand row of 4 flowers. You can now fill in the outside edges with the partial flowers for the corners and the sides.

Next, you are going to assemble the middle row of flowers by sewing 2 white hexagons between the top half flower on its finished side of 3 hexagons and the top of the first complete flower in that row. Continue joining the next 2 flowers and the bottom half flower in the same fashion until this row is complete. Then attach all 3 long rows together. No more white hexagons are needed at this point to fill in the space, because you have completed the rings on the outside rows. This quilt is backed and bound with a bright red calico.

This baby quilt can be increased to a full-sized quilt simply by adding more rows of flowers to fill it out. Each 3-ring flower makes approximately a 10-inch flower.

20
Grandmother's Flower Garden II

This crib quilt is slightly more complicated but very delicate looking when finished. It has a total of 909 pieces and is made of 1¼-inch hexagons. Its finished size is 28 × 37 inches. The flowers are made up of 7 hexagons—1 in the center and 6 around it. The hexagons making up the flowers are pastel prints. There are 53 flowers in the quilt for a total of 371 print hexagons; 538 white hexagons are needed to join the flowers. The top and bottom edges are scalloped; therefore, the quilt does not require any partial flowers.

To make this quilt, first make 53 flower hexagons. They should be separated into long rows for assembling; there will be 4 rows of 8 flowers and 3 rows of 7 flowers. Each of the long rows is joined by sewing 1 white hexagon between the top and bottom of each flower as shown. Then fill in on either side of this white hexagon with 2 white hexagons per side. Complete the circles around each of the flowers in the long rows as for Grandmother's Garden I. You then need to fill in the extra space or indentation between each flower on each of the outside edges of the rows with 1 more white hexagon. This takes 14 more white hexagons per long row. These long rows should now be even along the long sides and curved at the ends. The next step is to attach the short rows of 7 flowers to the long rows. First complete the shorter rows by attaching the 1 white hexagon between flowers and filling in with 2 on either side.

You are now ready to set the rows together. Look at the large illustration and notice how the flowers are staggered. Match up the white hexagons of the long rows to the white and colored hexagons on the shorter rows. After you have joined all 7 rows, you have to fill out the shorter rows with 3 more white hexagons at top and bottom.

This quilt is backed with pink cotton with a matching bias binding.

Quilting Pattern

For both Grandmother's Flower Garden I and II, the quilting pattern repeats the hexagon ⅛ inch inside the seam line of each piece.

Grandmother's Flower Garden crib quilt done in pastel
scrap fabrics joined with white and bound in pink. The
combination of the smaller hexagons, the pastel colors, and
the scalloped edges make a very delicate looking baby quilt.
Quilt made by Elizabeth Lippert Hinkel, courtesy Jo Hinkel.

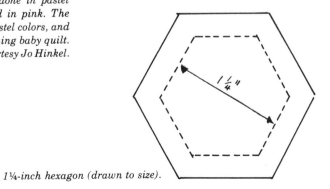

1¼-inch hexagon (drawn to size).

21
Windmill

This quilt has a finished dimension of 66 × 90, which is a good size for a twin-bed coverlet or blanket. Each block is 6 inches square and there are 117 blocks; 58 are patterned and 59 are plain. There is a 6-inch border all around, with a 6-inch white square pieced in each corner. There are 8 triangles per patterned square, for a total of 464 triangles and 527 pieces including the plain alternate and corner squares.

The quilt illustrated is made of two colors. White is used for the light triangles of the windmill and for the corners. The other triangles, as well as the alternating plain blocks and the border, are blue calico. Because of this color arrangement, there are really 2 patterns created in the top.

The Block

To assemble a patterned block, join 1 white and 1 blue triangle along their long sides to form a square. Complete 4 such squares. Then join the 4 squares so that white and blue alternate all around to form the windmill. Follow this same method to assemble all 58 patterned blocks.

The Set

There are 9 squares in the first row—5 plain and 4 patterned. Join these 9 squares, starting with a plain square and then alternating with a patterned and another plain across the whole row. Repeat this row 6 more times. The second row begins with a patterned block, then alternates with a plain followed by a patterned block until 9 squares have been joined to complete this row (5 patterned and 4 plain). Repeat this second row 5 more times.

When all the rows have been completed, assemble the rows. Alternate the odd-numbered rows that begin with plain blocks with the even-numbered rows that begin with patterned blocks.

Windmill quilt made in contrasting blue calico and white with patterned block alternating with plain calico square. There are two overall patterns created by the combination of colors and the set. The center of each windmill is tied with red yarn. Quilt courtesy the Caroli family.

Fabric Amounts

For the quilt illustrated, you need 232 white right triangles of a finished size of 3 inches per short side. You also need four 6-inch squares. For the white triangles and squares, you need 1¾ yards of 36-inch or 1½ yards of 45-inch fabric.

For the blue triangles, plain blocks, and unpieced borders, you need 6 yards of 36-inch or 4¾ yards of 45-inch fabric. If you cut only triangles of blue, you need 1½ yards of 36-inch or 1¼ yards of 45-inch fabric. If alternating squares are of a third color, you need 2½ yards of 36-inch or 2 yards of 45-inch fabric.

Quilting

The quilt illustrated is tied with red yarn in the center of every windmill. For more secure quilting, I suggest tying at the corners of every intersecting square as well.

For a traditional hand-quilting pattern, you could outline a windmill in every plain block and quilt inside the seam lines of the triangles in the patterned blocks.

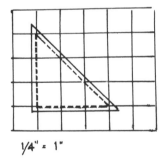

¼" = 1"

The Border

The borders are finished sizes of 6 × 54 for the top and bottom (cut 7 × 55 for ½-inch seam allowances) and 6 × 78 (cut 7 × 79) for the long sides. These borders are attached to each side of the quilt and then pieced at the corners with 6-inch white squares.

22
Birds in Flight Variation

This triangle quilt has a finished size of 84 × 96. The only pattern piece is a right triangle. A total of 836 triangles (418 light and 418 dark) are needed for this quilt. Even though so many pieces are needed, this is a simple quilt to make. Two triangles (1 light and 1 dark) are joined along their long sides to form a square. This can be done on the sewing machine, since only 1 side is stitched at a time and the shortest sides are a finished length of 4 inches. There are 19 rows of 4-inch squares across the quilt and 22 lengthwise. A 4-inch border of a neutral print is added on all sides.

The first step in making this quilt is to make 418 squares by sewing 1 light and 1 dark triangle together along their long sides. These squares are then sewn into long rows or strips, always keeping the light triangles on the same side of the square. Then join the long strips being careful of two things: first, that the light sides of the squares stay on the same side throughout, and secondly, that each seam line is matched precisely with the seam lines in the row above and below. If any of the seams are not perfectly matched, the finished quilt top will show it quite clearly.

Fabric Amounts

For the light triangles, you need a total of 4¼ yards of 36-inch or 3¾ yards of 45-inch light-colored fabric. You need the same amounts of dark fabric. If you buy ½-yard lots you can cut 42 triangles from each 36-inch width and need 10 light pieces and 10 dark pieces of fabric. From 45-inch fabric, you can cut 48 triangles from ½ yard. You need 9 light and 9 dark fabrics.

Quilting

The most effective pattern is to repeat the pattern of triangles inside each piece ¼ inch in from the seam. Intersecting straight lines, which form squares, can be repeated in the border. Since the border is only 4 inches wide, it does not have to be quilted.

Birds in Flight quilt has a simple 3-inch triangle as the only pattern piece. The striking light and dark contrasts are achieved in random scraps of printed fabrics by using very light prints attached to quite dark prints. Quilt courtesy of the Caroli family.

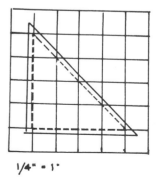

1/4" = 1"

23
Lone Star

The finished dimensions of this quilt are 80 × 96. The basic pattern piece is a diamond of 4 inches per side. You need a total of 288 diamonds. The background is filled in by piecing background fabric to fit between the points of the star after the star is assembled. The star is made of 8 large pieced diamonds of 36 small diamonds each. The finished star plus the background filler pieces is 80 × 80. Two strips of background fabric, each 8 × 80 (finished size), are added one to the top and one to the bottom to complete the top.

The Block

The basic block is a large diamond of 11 rows. In the quilt illustrated, the first row is 1 red diamond. The second row is 2 red and white polka-dot diamonds. Row 3 is 3 diamonds of red and blue paisley print; row 4 is 4 diamonds of solid blue; row 5 is 5 diamonds of red and white paisley; row 6 is 6 diamonds of navy blue. Row 7 repeats row 5; row 8 repeats row 4; row 9 repeats row 3; row 10 repeats row 2; and row 11 repeats row 1.

To assemble a block, join rows 1 and 2 as follows. Sew one side of the polka-dot diamond to one of the bottom sides of a red diamond. Sew the second polka-dot diamond to the other bottom side of the red diamond so that the point of the red diamond is centered between the two points of the polka-dot diamonds. Join row 3 through row 6 following this same procedure. Row 6 is the center and widest row of the diamond. The next 5 rows are added by decreasing 1 diamond per row and setting the points of each new row exactly between two sides of diamonds in the preceding row.

These sides must be pieced exactly so that the points of alternating rows meet exactly at all four points.

Fabric Amounts

Of navy blue you need: 1¼ yards of 36-inch or 1 yard of 45-inch fabric. Of red and white paisley you need 2 yards of 36-inch or 1¾ yards of 45-inch fabric. Of solid blue you need 1¾ yards of 36-inch or 1¼ yards of 45-inch fabric. Of red and blue paisley you need 1¼ yards of 36-inch or 1 yard of 45-inch fabric. Of red and white polka dot you need ¾ yard of 36-inch or 45-inch fabric. Of red you need ½ yard of 36-inch or 45-inch fabric. In summary, you need to cut 48 navy-blue, 80 red and white paisley, 64 solid blue, 48 red and blue paisley, 32 red and white polka-dot, and 16 red diamonds.

The Set

To assemble the whole star, lay out the 8 large diamonds and follow the same principle for joining smaller diamonds. Make sure you match the edges of each color to the same color of the other large diamond. In other words, the navy-blue row of 1 large diamond joins the navy-blue row of the next large diamond. You begin with navy-blue rows and end with a red row. As you can see in the large illustration, only ½ of the large diamonds are joined.

Quilting

Each diamond is quilted ¼ inch inside each seam line. Between the points of top and bottom and sides, quilt parallel straight lines to fill in the plain areas of the quilt.

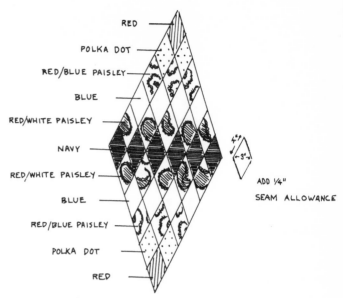

To complete ⅛ of finished star, assemble eleven rows of diamonds, following the pattern indicated in the drawing. When eight of these large diamonds have been completed, they should be sewn together by joining bottom halves of each diamond to the next one. Take special care to match points and seam lines of smaller diamonds to make the finished star turn out correctly. It is a bit easier to be exact if you complete four diamonds or half of the finished star at a time and then join the two halves as the last step.

This Lone Star quilt is made up of diamonds 4 inches per side exactly like the main pattern piece of Baby Blocks. Quilt courtesy Paul Rueckwald, Flower in the Crannied Wall.

24
Six-pointed Stars

The finished dimensions of this quilt are 72 × 92. It consists of 18 pieced stars appliquéd to 14-inch foundation blocks, which are set together with 1-inch lattice strips on the diagonal. There are 10 large white triangles, which are half the finished size of the foundation blocks, and 4 white corner triangles to fill in the sides. A 4-inch border of fabric matching the lattice strips is added on all sides to finish the quilt.

For these large-sized pieces, such as the 14-inch squares and the lattice strips, use ½-inch seam allowances for ease in sewing. Also use ½-inch seam allowance for the borders.

The Block

Each block consists of a 6-pointed star made up of 6 diamonds of 4 inches per side. (The pattern for the diamond in the Baby Blocks quilt can be used for this quilt.) Each star is of two colors arranged in alternating diamonds. Once the star is assembled, it is then appliquéd to a square. Take care to line up the points of each star with corners and be sure to center each star exactly on its foundation block as shown in the illustration. The stars can be pieced on the sewing machine, since the sides are 4 inches long. But be especially careful to match the points exactly at the center of the star, as well as at the ends of each seam.

The Set

The quilt is set together with 1-inch lattice strips, and the blocks are joined diagonally. Use 10 triangles to fill in the sides and the top and bottom, plus 4 corner triangles. First set together 2 long rows of 5 blocks each diagonally, as shown in illustration, using 4 short lattice strips of finished dimensions of 1 × 15 (cut 2 × 16 for ½-inch seam allowance). Then add a lattice strip to each end of each row. (This is 4 more lattice strips.)

Next, set in the top-right corner triangle on one row and the bottom-left corner triangle to the other row. There will be 4 corner right triangles in all, each of which should be a finished size of 11 inches per short side and 16 inches on the long side.

Next, set in place 1 side triangle at opposite ends of each long row (opposite from the corner pieces already added). These larger triangles have a finished size of 15 inches per short side and 21 for the long side. The two long rows are then joined together with the longest lattice strip, which is 1 × 91 finished (2 × 92 cutting size). Now add the 2 next longest lattice strips (1 × 76 finished, 2 × 77 cutting size) to each side of the joined rows.

Complete 2 more rows of a large-sized triangle followed by 3 star blocks and 1 more side triangle; each 2 pieces should be joined by short lattice strips. Then add each of these rows to each side of the long center rows, using the 2 remaining long lattice strips of 1 × 46 finished size (2 × 47 cutting size).

To finish the pattern of the top, assemble each corner. Again following the illustration, assemble lattice strips and triangle to 3 sides of each of the last 2 star blocks. Then attach the lattice-strip edge of the rows of 3 star blocks at top left and bottom right of the quilt. When you are laying out the star blocks for joining, mark the sides in some fashion so that you will have each star placed at the proper angle to make all

the stars in the finished top point in the same direction. Finally, attach the border strips, mitering the corners.

Fabric Amounts

To sum up the pattern pieces needed: 108 diamonds to form the 18 stars, eighteen 14-inch foundation squares, 10 large triangles, 4 corner triangles, 26 short lattice strips (cut 2 × 16), 5 long lattice strips (1 cut 2 × 92; 2 cut 2 × 77; and 2 cut 2 × 47).

If all the stars are made alike with 2 colors for each, you need 1¾ yards of 36-inch or 1¼ yards of 45-inch fabric for diamonds. If you use random fabrics as in the quilt shown, you need 36 scraps of ¼ yard each. For lattice strips and borders, you need 2¾ yards of 36-inch or 45-inch fabric for unpieced borders and lattice strips. For the white muslin foundation blocks and triangles, you need 6 yards of 36-inch or 45-inch fabric.

Quilting Pattern

The quilting pattern for this quilt is similar to the Baby Blocks previously described. Each diamond is quilted ¼ inch in from the seam line. Then 4 diamonds are quilted within each pieced diamond. Each lattice strip is quilted ½ inch inside its seam line. The rest of the quilt is quilted in diagonal parallel lines 1 inch apart in both diagonal directions so that 1-inch squares are formed over the top.

This individual six-pointed star quilt is made of brightly contrasting colors. Each star has 3 solid-color diamonds and 3 printed diamonds of either contrasting or complementing colors. The basic pattern piece is a diamond of 4 inches per side, exactly the same pattern piece as in the Lone Star the Baby Blocks quilts. Quilt made by Lina Duckworth Williams, courtesy Byron Williams, Jr.

25
Biscuit

This quilt is also sometimes called a "puff quilt" or "gathered patchwork." Each block is really a complete little quilt in itself. The quilt illustrated has a finished size of 36 × 54, excluding the lace edging. There are 6 blocks across and 9 down for a total of 54 blocks. Each block is made up of 2 different-sized squares, for a total of 108 pieces for the whole quilt.

These quilts can be made as large as you like simply by enlarging the squares or by increasing the number of rows across and/or down. In this quilt, the squares are 6 inches when finished. Cut the back squares 6½ × 6½ and the top squares 8½ × 8½. Use 6 colors, all ginghams. Sew the large top to the smaller bottom squares. Take 2 tucks on each side to take in the fullness of the top piece, so that when sewn together, the outside edges of each square align. This fuller top square creates the "puff," which will be stuffed. To join squares, place wrong sides of fabric together and seam on 3 sides. On the fourth side, leave an opening large enough to stuff polyester fiberfill through; stuff the square; then blind stitch the opening closed. This is a very good quilt to make on the sewing machine.

Complete all 54 squares. Then lay out to plan the arrangement of colors. Stitch long rows by matching the seams between blocks carefully. Sew the rows together.

Add a 1½-inch lace edging and a backing. To join the backing to the finished top, machine stitch the right sides together on 3 sides, with the lace between backing and top. Then turn inside out like a pillowcase and blind stitch the fourth side.

Fabric Amounts

You need 2¼ yards of 36-inch or 1¾ yards of 45-inch fabric for the small back squares. This can be any fabric, since it won't be seen in the finished quilt. I generally use muslin.

You need 3½ yards total of 36-inch and 2¾ yards total of 45-inch fabric to cut the 8½-inch top squares. Of course, you must use at least 4 different fabrics to vary the colors of the top.

One-half yard of 36-inch fabric will cut ten 6½-inch squares or eight 8½-inch squares. One-half yard of 45-inch fabric will cut twelve 6½-inch squares or ten 8½-inch squares.

Finish by tying every few squares with ties showing on back or front. Or you can secure with embroidery stitches showing on the back.

This Biscuit quilt is made for a crib, but can be made any size either by enlarging the size of the squares, by increasing the numbers of squares, or by a combination of the two methods. This quilt is made from a combination of five different pastel ginghams for a child's room. Quilt courtesy Kimberly Heather Rogers.

26
Animal Babies Crib Quilt

This crib quilt has a finished size of 47 × 63. There are 47 pieces in the quilt. It consists of twelve 14-inch squares, each with a different animal appliquéd to a white foundation block. The blocks are joined with 17 short lattice strips, which in turn are joined with 6 small white squares. The outside edges are bound with a 1-inch binding. The 12 animals are each cut from a different printed cotton and detailed with embroidery stitches for facial features, etc. Each animal is lightly stuffed when it is appliquéd to its background square.

The quilt should be made as follows. First cut out the animals: 1 giraffe, 1 whale, 1 puppy, 1 mouse, 1 duck, 1 seal, 1 monkey, 1 chicken, 1 rabbit, 1 kitten, 1 elephant, and 1 pig. You need a 14-inch square of fabric for each animal. Appliqué each animal to its foundation square, stuffing lightly, and embroider the features of each animal.

The Set

Join the 3 long rows by sewing the 4 blocks together with 3 lattice strips between joining blocks. You need 17 lattice strips each 2½ × 14½ (allowing ¼ inch for seam allowance on all sides). The long rows are assembled as follows:

Row 1: Giraffe, lattice strip, mouse, lattice strip, monkey, lattice strip, kitten.

Row 2: Whale, lattice strip, duck, lattice strip, chicken, lattice strip, elephant.

Row 3: Puppy, lattice strip, seal, lattice strip, rabbit, lattice strip, pig.

After these long rows are attached, sew 4 lattice strips to the right side of row 1 and to the right side of row 2, matching corners carefully. Next on row 1 attach three 2-inch squares in place on 3 sides to attach lattice strips, being very careful to sew even seams. Then sew the 3 squares for the lattice strips attached to row 2. Join rows 1 and 2, and finally, attach row 3, again being very careful to match seams and corners.

Fabric Amounts

You need 2¾ yards of 36-inch or 1¾ yards of 45-inch white fabric for background squares and 2-inch squares (cut 2½ inches) for lattice strips; twelve 14-inch squares of various prints for the animals; ¾ yard of 36-inch or ½ yard of 45-inch calico for the lattice strips.

Quilting

Each animal is outlined with quilting stitches ⅛ inch from the appliqué line.

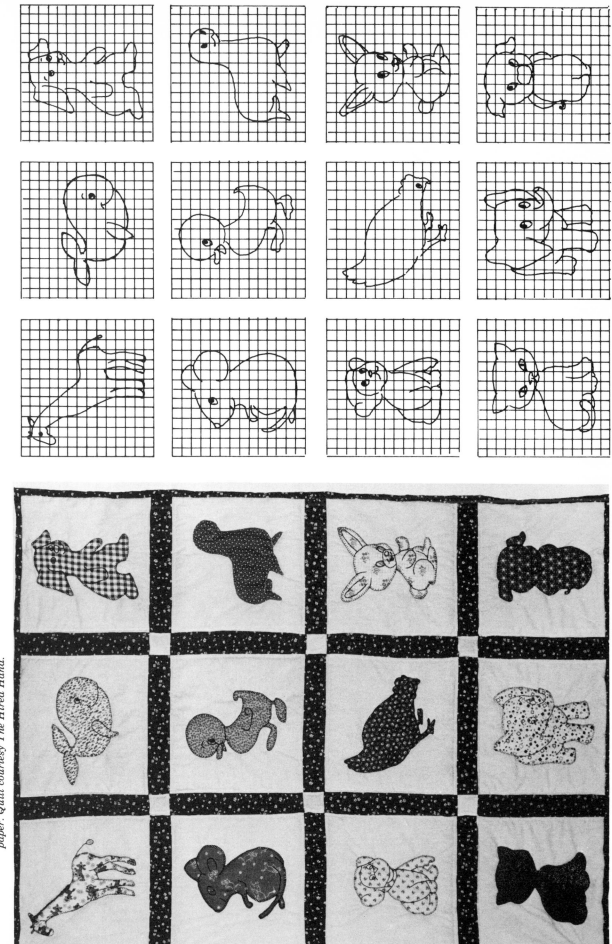

Animal Babies crib quilt with each square featuring a different calico animal embellished with embroidery stitches for detail. The pattern pieces given can be enlarged to whatever size you desire by redrawing on graph paper. Quilt courtesy The Hired Hand.

⅛" = 1"

27
Sunbonnet Sue and Farmer Bill

This delightful crib quilt has a finished size of 40 × 50 with 8-inch background squares joined by 2-inch lattice strips and a 6-inch border, both of a bright calico print. A total of 71 pieces is needed.

There are two characters in this appliqué quilt, Sunbonnet Sue and Farmer Bill. Sue requires 3 pieces to complete her figure—1 for her dress, 1 for her bonnet, and 1 for her feet. Bill requires 5 pieces to complete his figure—1 for his overalls, 2 for his shirt, 1 for his hat, and 1 for his feet. After each figure is appliquéd onto its background square, the details of the design are embroidered on, using primarily an outline stitch to indicate hatbands, arms, legs, etc. Further embroidery embellishments, like flowers for Sue and fishing poles for Bill, are sometimes added. In the very elaborate interpretations of this design, each figure in the quilt is engaged in a different activity like hoeing a garden, raking leaves, flying a kite, baking bread, etc. In this quilt, there are 6 blocks of Sunbonnet Sue and 6 blocks of Farmer Bill.

The Set

The quilt is set together with 2-inch-wide calico lattice strips between each block, and it is finished with a 6-inch border of the same calico as the lattice strips. Decide on the preferred arrangement of the figures by laying out the appliquéd squares. The quilt shown has 2 Sues with 1 Bill in the middle for the first and third rows, and 2 Bills with 1 Sue in the middle for the second and last rows. After you have settled on the arrangement, join the blocks that make up the long rows with short lattice strips. These strips should be cut 2½ × 8½ inches long to allow a ¼-inch seam allowance on all sides. The finished dimensions are 2 × 8 inches. Then join the long rows together with the long lattice strips, very carefully matching the cross strips. These long strips should be 2½ × 39 inches unfinished (2 × 38 finished). Then add the border on all 4 sides.

Fabric Amounts

You need 2½ yards of 36-inch or 1¾ yards of 45-inch calico for unpieced borders and the lattice strips. You need much less fabric if you piece the borders. For the background squares, you need ¾ yard of white muslin. To complete the figures of the children you need fabric as follows:

one 18-inch square of dark fabric for shoes.
one 18-inch square for Bill's hats (traditionally dark-yellow to represent straw).
six 4-inch squares for Bill's shirts.
six 6-inch squares for Bill's overalls.
six 9-inch squares for Sue's dresses and sunbonnets.

Sunbonnet Sue and Farmer Bill appliquéd child's quilt, set together with calico lattice strips to match the borders. Each figure has a different costume. This is a very popular and traditional subject for children's quilts. Quilt courtesy The Hired Hand.

(In the quilt illustrated, Sue wears matching dress and bonnet, but if you wish them to be different, plan for twelve 6-inch squares.)

Quilting

The quilting pattern first outlines each figure. It then forms straight lines around each square just inside the seams of each lattice strip. Within each square is a diagonal straight line pattern of 9 lines across each block. The border is quilted with 4 rows of parallel lines in the direction of the border. Each quilting row turns a corner to join its cross row at a right angle, creating an overall effect of concentric squares framing the whole quilt.

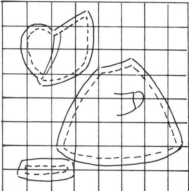

1/4" = 1"

28
Rosebud Wreath Appliqué

This is a beautiful and somewhat elaborate quilt. Its finished size is 80 × 80. Each block has a finished size of 20 inches square and contains 33 pieces. There are 16 blocks. The total number of pieces for the quilt is 528.

There are 7 different pieces for this quilt: 1 stem, cut from 1-inch-wide bias tape, 44 inches long; 4 flowers of 4-inch diameters; 4 flower centers of 1½-inch diameters; 8 buds, approximately 1¾-inches per side of triangle; 4 triangular bud cases, approximately 4 inches long and 3½ inches wide at the bud end; 4 curved bud cases, approximately 4 inches long and 3¼ inches wide at the bud case; and 8 leaves, about 1½ inches at the widest point by 3 inches at the longest point. All measurements are finished sizes. When cutting, add ¼ inch per edge for seam allowances.

This makes a total of 16 stems, 64 flowers, 64 flower centers, 128 buds, 64 triangular bud cases, 64 rounded bud cases, and 128 leaves.

The Block

To form each block, first appliqué the circular stem in place, centering it carefully. Next, position the triangular bud cases to the outside of the stem so that they point exactly to the 4 corners. Leave the bud ends open. The curved bud piece goes down next on the inside of the stem, pointing exactly toward the opposite corners and leaving the bud end open. The stem ends on the bud cases are tucked under the stem. The buds are then tucked under the edges of the bud cases, and the buds and open ends of the cases are appliquéd.

Now stitch down the 4 flowers, centering them exactly between the buds. The flowers are sewn over the stem. The centers of the flowers are appliquéd over the flowers. Finally, the leaves are appliquéd on. Each leaf should be positioned halfway between a bud and a flower on the outside of the wreath.

The colors in the quilt illustrated are wonderful. The leaves, stems, and bud cases are olive green; the flowers are pale peach with darker centers, except for the top row where the flowers are dark red. The bottom 3 rows of the quilt have all red buds except for one square that has peach buds. The buds in the top row are mostly red.

This quilt was appliquéd by machine, using a top stitch ⅛ inch from the edge of each piece.

Rosebud Wreath machine appliquéd quilt made of dark green, peach, and dark red on a white background. Quilt courtesy Paul Rueckwald, Flower in the Crannied Wall.

The Border

This border is a lovely variation of a Saw-tooth border. It is made up of alternate orange and white triangles 2½ inches wide at the base and 3½ inches on each side. The orange triangles are curved at the bases for a finished length of 4 inches. Since they form the outside edge, they give the quilt a scalloped border. To complete this border, you need 128 white triangles and 136 orange triangles.

To assemble the border, begin and end each of the lengthwise rows with an orange triangle—there will be 33 orange and 32 white triangles in each of these 2 rows. For the top and bottom borders of the quilt, also begin and end each row with orange triangles; there will be 33 orange and 32 white triangles in each of these border strips. Where the borders meet at the corners of the quilt, piece 1 single orange triangle to fill the space.

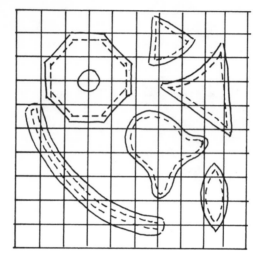

1/4" = 1"

Index